According to Your Word

Portrait of Cardinal Connell by Conor Walton,
courtesy of Archbishop's House, Dublin

According to Your Word

Proceedings of a conference held on Saturday 4 March 2006
at the Pontifical Irish College Rome to honour

DESMOND CARDINAL CONNELL

on his eightieth birthday

Liam Bergin

EDITOR

FOUR COURTS PRESS

Set in 11 on 15 Adobe Garamond for
FOUR COURTS PRESS LTD
7 Malpas Street, Dublin 8, Ireland
e-mail: info@fourcourtspress.ie
http://www.fourcourtspress.ie
and in North America
FOUR COURTS PRESS
c/o ISBS, 920 N.E. 58th Avenue, Suite 300, Portland, OR 97213.

© The various contributors and Four Courts Press 2007

ISBN 978–1–84682–083–0

SPECIAL ACKNOWLEDGMENT
The publication of this book was generously supported by the Pontifical Irish College, Rome.

Printed in England by
MPG Books, Bodmin, Cornwall

Contents

Illustrations

Acknowledgments

THIS BOOK IS PUBLISHED in honour of Cardinal Desmond Connell as he celebrated his eightieth birthday on 24 March 2006. The first part contains the papers delivered at a conference organised by the Pontifical Irish College to mark this event. The second part presents essays from a number of disciplines by people who are associated both with Cardinal Connell and with the Pontifical Irish College.

I wish to thank all who contributed to the conference and to this volume. The generosity of the staff and students at the Pontifical Irish College who organised this event is greatly appreciated.

Titian's *Noli me tangere* is reproduced with permission of the National Gallery, London.

LIAM BERGIN

Contributors

LIAM BERGIN is a priest of the diocese of Ossory and rector of the Pontifical Irish College. He also lectures in dogmatic theology at the Pontifical Gregorian University in Rome. After taking a science degree in Saint Patrick's College, Maynooth, he studied theology at the Gregorian. He was awarded the Bellarmine Prize by the Gregorian University for his doctoral thesis which was published as *O profeticum lavacrum: Baptism as prophetic act* (Rome, 1998). He is the editor of *Faith, word and culture* (Dublin, 2004) and has contributed articles to a number of journals.

THOMAS G. CASEY is an Irish Jesuit priest from Dublin and professor of philosophy at the Pontifical Gregorian University in Rome. Previously he taught at Belvedere College in Dublin, as well as lecturing at Milltown Institute, and working as a chaplain to university students. He has a licentiate in theology from Weston School of Theology in Cambridge, Massachusetts, a licentiate in philosophy from Milltown Institute, an MLitt in philosophy from the Sorbonne, and a PhD in philosophy from University College Dublin. He has published three books; the most recent is *Music of pure love* (Illinois, 2006). His articles have appeared in *The Furrow, Studies, The Way, Review for Religious, La Civiltà Cattolica, America* and *Gregorianum.*

MICHAEL G. DUIGNAN is a priest of the diocese of Elphin. As a student at the Pontifical Irish College, he undertook his philosophical and theological formation at the Gregorian University, Rome. He defended his doctoral thesis in 2006 with a dissertation entitled *The trinitarian theology of Catholic authors: a comparative study of the work of William J. Hill, Walter Kasper, Anthony Kelly and Catherine Mowery LaCugna* (Rome, 2006). He is lecturer and co-ordinator of various programmes in religious education and theology at Saint Angela's College, Sligo, an affiliated college of the National University of Ireland, Galway.

BRIAN FARRELL was born in Dublin, Ireland in 1944. In 1961 he entered the congregation of the Legionaries of Christ, one of the first Irish members of the community founded in 1941 in Mexico by Father Marcial Maciel. From 1961 to 1963 Bishop Farrell studied at the congregation's novitiate and house of studies at Salamanca, Spain. He continued his training at the Gregorian University, Rome, and in the United States, and was ordained to the priesthood in Rome in November 1969. After ordination, Bishop Farrell worked to establish the Legionaries of Christ in the United States and for a number of years was director of the congregation's house of formation in Connecticut. In 1978 he began doctoral studies at the Gregorian University, Rome, obtaining a doctorate in theology in 1983 with a thesis entitled 'Communicatio in sacris: a theological study of the policy adopted by the Second Vatican Council'. In the meantime, in 1981, he entered the Secretariat of State, and in the 1990s became department head of the English-language Section. On 19 December 2002 he was named titular bishop of Abitinae and appointed secretary of the Pontifical Council for Promoting Christian Unity. He was ordained bishop by Pope John Paul II in Saint Peter's basilica on 6 January 2003.

SEAN FERNANDEZ, a priest of the archdiocese of Perth, is senior lecturer in the college of philosophy and theology at the University of Notre Dame Australia, Fremantle, Western Australia, and parish priest of Attadale in Western Australia. He has previously taught theology at the Pontifical Gregorian University. He took his first theological degree at Flinders University, Adelaide. He has a licence in sacred theology (fundamental theology) and a doctorate in sacred theology (dogmatic theology) from the Pontifical Gregorian University. His doctoral thesis was entitled 'The doctrine of God according to Cornelius Ernst, Herbert McCabe and Nicholas Lash'. While pursuing postgraduate studies he was at the Pontifical Irish College, Rome and, for periods, at Magdalene College, Cambridge.

MICHAEL PAUL GALLAGHER, an Irish Jesuit priest, entered religious life after studying literature at universities in Ireland and France. He did research in literature and theology at Oxford, Johns Hopkins, and Queen's

University, Belfast. From 1972 to 1990 he lectured in English literature at University College Dublin. From 1990 to 1995 he worked in the Vatican in the Pontifical Council for Culture. Since 1995 he has been professor of fundamental theology at the Gregorian University, Rome, where he became dean of the faculty of theology in 2005. He has published some ten books of spiritual or pastoral theology, the most recent being: *Dive deeper: the human poetry of faith* (2001) and *Clashing symbols: an introduction to faith and culture* (revised edition, 2003).

EILEEN KANE was formerly senior lecturer in history of art in University College Dublin. She was educated at the Dominican College, Eccles Street, Dublin, and at University College, Dublin, where she took the degrees of BA and MA, and the Higher Diploma in Education. She was awarded the degree of PhD for her thesis on the Avignonese painter Jacques Yverni, and painting in south-eastern France and Piedmont in the early fifteenth century. Her research interests and her publications have centred upon art in Avignon, Rome (especially the basilica of San Clemente) and Dublin. Her most recent book (2005) is *The Church of San Silvestro in Capite in Rome*, the titular church of His Eminence Cardinal Connell. In 2000, Dr Kane was conferred with the papal honour of Dame of the Order of Pope Saint Gregory the Great.

BREANDÁN LEAHY was born in 1960 in Dublin and was ordained a priest for his home diocese in 1986. After his studies both in law at University College Dublin and King's Inn and in philosophy at Holy Cross College, Dublin, he began theology at the Gregorian University, Rome, residing from 1983 to 1986 at the Irish College. His doctoral thesis is entitled *The Marian principle in the ecclesiological writings of Hans Urs von Balthasar* (Frankfurt, 1996). His work, *The Marian profile* (London and New York, 2000) has been translated into Italian, Spanish and Portuguese. He has taught theology at Clonliffe College, the Mater Dei Institute, the Irish School of Ecumenics, Dublin and Edgehill Methodist College, Belfast. Currently, he is professor of systematic theology at Saint Patrick's College, Maynooth.

WILLIAM JOSEPH LEVADA was ordained to the priesthood in Saint Peter's Basilica in 1961. He was subsequently engaged in pastoral ministry in parishes and taught theology at Saint John's Seminary School of Theology, located at Camarillo in the archdiocese of Los Angeles. In 1976, he was appointed an official of the Congregation for the Doctrine of the Faith in the Vatican. During his six years of service, he continued teaching theology part-time as an instructor at the Pontifical Gregorian University. He was named auxiliary bishop of Los Angeles, and was ordained titular bishop of Capri on 12 May 1983. On 1 July 1986, he was appointed eighth archbishop of Portland, Oregon. During his nine years in Portland, Archbishop Levada was able to devote time to the recruitment of priestly vocations and enhancement of the seminary at Mt. Angel, where he taught ecclesiology. Appointed coadjutor archbishop of San Francisco on 17 August 1995, Archbishop Levada was installed on 24 October that year, and succeeded Archbishop John Quinn, as seventh archbishop of San Francisco on 27 December 1995. From 1986 to 1993 he served as the only American bishop on the editorial committee of the Vatican commission for the *Catechism of the Catholic Church*. During 2000, he was designated bishop co-chair of the Anglican–Roman Catholic dialogue in the United States (ARC–USA). In November 2000, he was appointed a member of the Congregation of the Doctrine of the Faith. On 13 May 2005, Pope Benedict XVI appointed Archbishop Levada Prefect of the Congregation for the Doctrine of the Faith. He was created cardinal in the consistory of 25 March 2006 and was assigned the diaconal title of Santa Maria in Domnica. Cardinal Levada also serves as president of the International Theological Commission and the Pontifical Biblical Commission.

DIARMUID MARTIN was ordained a priest of the archdiocese of Dublin in 1969. He later pursued higher studies in moral theology at the Angelicum University in Rome. Having served in parochial ministry in Dublin, he was responsible for the pastoral care of Dublin pilgrims during the 1975 holy year in Rome. He entered the service of the Holy See in 1976 in the Pontifical Council for the Family. In 1986 he was appointed under-secretary at the Pontifical Council for Justice and Peace and, in 1994, secretary of the same pontifical council. In 1998 he was appointed titular bishop of

Glendalough and was ordained by Pope John Paul II on 6 January 1999. In March 2001 he was elevated to the rank of archbishop and became permanent observer of the Holy See at the United Nations in Geneva. He was appointed as coadjutor archbishop of Dublin in 2003 and became archbishop in 2004.

ANDREW G. MCGRADY is registrar of the Mater Dei Institute of Education, Dublin. His academic background is the field of education with a particular interest in the areas of religious education, the religious, spiritual and ethical dimensions of full human development, Catholic schooling world-wide and comparative education.

JOSEPH MURPHY was born in Cork in 1968. He obtained a Bachelor of Arts degree in French and Mathematics at Saint Patrick's College, Maynooth, in 1989, before studying for the baccalaureate and subsequently the licence in sacred theology from the Pontifical Gregorian University, Rome. Ordained a priest for the diocese of Cloyne in 1993, he entered the service of the Holy See in 1997, where he is presently an official of the section for relations with states of the Secretariat of State. He has published articles in the *Irish Theological Quarterly* and in the French journal *Kephas*. A book on the theology of Pope Benedict XVI, entitled *An invitation to joy: the theological vision of Pope Benedict XVI*, is forthcoming from Ignatius Press, San Francisco.

FRAN O'ROURKE is senior lecturer in the School of Philosophy, University College Dublin. He studied in Galway, Vienna, Leuven, Cologne and Munich. He has published widely on Plato, Aristotle, Neoplatonism, Aquinas and Heidegger. He is former director of the UCD International Summer School for Irish Studies. In 1992 he edited *At the heart of the real*, a Festschrift in honour of Archbishop Desmond Connell. His book *Pseudo-Dionysius and the metaphysics of Aquinas*, described by Alasdair MacIntyre as 'one of the two or three most important books on Aquinas published in the last fifty years,' was reprinted by University of Notre Dame Press in 2005. His monograph, *'Allwisest Stagyrite': Joyce's quotations from Aristotle*, was recently published by the National Library of Ireland.

ANGELO SODANO was ordained a priest for the diocese of Asti in 1950. He taught dogmatic theology at the diocesan seminary before entering the Pontificia Accademia Ecclesiastica in 1959. He subsequently served in apostolic nunciatures in Ecuador, Uruguay and Chile. Following a period in the Roman Curia from 1968 to 1977, he was nominated titular archbishop of Nova di Caesare and apostolic nuncio in Chile. In 1988 he was appointed secretary of the then Council for the Public Affairs of the Church; in 1989 he became secretary for relations with states. He was appointed pro-secretary of state in 1990. He was created a cardinal and appointed secretary of state by Pope John Paul II in June 1991. He was appointed dean of the college of cardinals and cardinal-bishop of Ostia by Pope Benedict XVI in 2005.

LINDA ZAGZEBSKI holds the Kingfisher Chair of the Philosophy of Religion and Ethics in the Department of Philosophy in the University of Oklahoma. Currently president of the Society of Christian Philosophers, Professor Zagzebski was president of the American Catholic Philosophical Association in 1997–98. Her publications include six books and more than 60 journal articles. Professor Zagzebski's latest work, *Philosophy of religion: an historical introduction*, will be published in 2007 by Blackwell.

Introduction

LIAM BERGIN

Your Eminence Cardinal Connell,
Your Excellency Ambassador McDonagh, the Irish Ambassador to
    the Holy See,
Your Excellency Ambassador Cogan, the Irish Ambassador to Italy,
Archbishop Martin,
Archbishop Monterisi,
Bishop Farrell.

I T IS INDEED A PRIVILEGE for the Pontifical Irish College to welcome
you here today to honour Desmond Cardinal Connell as his eightieth
birthday approaches. Born in Dublin on 24 March 1926, Desmond
Connell was the second of three sons who survived infancy. Ordained a
priest of the archdiocese of Dublin in 1951; professor of general metaphysics
in University College Dublin in 1972; archbishop of Dublin in 1988;
cardinal priest of San Silvestro in Capite in 2001. A short biography of
Cardinal Connell is to be found on the back of the programme for today's
events so there is no need to repeat it all.

The Pontifical Irish College is honoured to host this event for a
number of reasons. First of all – history. Without Dublin and without the
generosity of the archbishops of Dublin this college would not exist.
Founded in 1628, it was suppressed in 1798 during the Napoleonic occupa-
tion of Rome. In 1824, Michael Blake, vicar general of Dublin, was allowed
to resign his parish and come to Rome to re-found the college in 1826. Task
completed, he returned to his parish in 1828 only to be appointed bishop of
Dromore a few years later. Paul Cullen was rector of the college from 1832
to 1849. As archbishop of Dublin and Ireland's first cardinal he saw the
college and the church in Ireland through the trauma of the famine and its
aftermath. This particular house was founded by another Dublin priest,

John Hagan who was rector from 1919 to 1930. Only yesterday did we see a five-minute film of Hagan and his Dublin vice-rector and successor Michael Curran, as they surveyed this site together with a figure that seems to be Archbishop Byrne as the building was under construction.

The Dublin men weren't just builders and shakers. They were holy men too. One, Joseph Columba Marmion who was ordained here in 1881 for the archdiocese of Dublin, was beatified by Pope John Paul II in September 2000.

The archbishop of Dublin is also a trustee of the Irish College and his support and interest in the affairs of the college are vital. Dublin has always been generous to the Irish College – a recent gift to enable cataloguing in the archive bears that out. Dublin has been and is generous to us; it is only fitting that today we acknowledge that and attempt something in return.

In recent years, with his appointment as a member to the Pontifical Council for Migrants, and to the Pontifical Council for the Laity as well as to the Congregations for the Doctrine of the Faith and for Bishops, Cardinal Connell has spent a lot of time in Rome and in this house. The interest he takes in each seminarian and priest who lives here is striking. He has felt at home here and we have appreciated his paternal presence. Families don't let birthdays pass unmarked. Neither could we.

But there is a great coincidence, maybe it is providence. Not only does Cardinal Connell celebrate his eightieth birthday; so too does this building. Both were born in 1926. Now the cardinal was remarking the fact that his legs aren't what they used to be. Eminence, I'd like to assure you that you have emerged from these eighty years with considerably less scaffolding than our perimeter wall and courtyard at the moment!

Our programme today is in three parts: philosophical, theological and ecclesiological. The three parts reflect and celebrate three important periods in Cardinal Connell's life. The first, the philosophical, honours the cardinal philosopher; the second, the theological, honours the cardinal pastor; the third, the ecclesiological, honours the cardinal teacher. There will be a break for some forty minutes for a reception between parts two and three. Our afternoon ends with first vespers of the first Sunday of advent. Joining our own students in singing the psalms we are happy to welcome the participation of the choir from the Teutonic College which counts three Dublin priests in its ranks.

The first part of our gathering is entitled 'The beautiful dangers of being.' I would like to introduce Dr Eileen Kane who has kindly agreed to chair this section. Eileen Kane is a former lecturer on the history of art in University College Dublin. She was a member of the Dublin Diocesan Heritage Commission and is evangelical in her zeal to ensure that seminarians and priests have some appreciation of the religious and cultural heritage that often comes within their care. In 2000, Dr Kane was conferred with the papal honour of Dame of the Order of Pope Saint Gregory the Great. Last year Dr Kane published a work on the history of San Silvestro, Cardinal Connell's titular church here in Rome.

'According to your word'

EILEEN KANE

'According to your word'. Those are the words which we saw immediately upon entering the Pontifical Irish College today, in response to the very gracious invitation of the rector, Monsignor Liam Bergin. *Secundum verbum tuum* – according to your word. Those are the words spoken by Mary in response to the most gracious and greatest invitation ever issued, words spoken in fullness of faith, and trust and readiness to serve.

Since his appointment as archbishop of Dublin in January 1988, Cardinal Desmond Connell has made those words his motto, but one imagines that they were already his own, spoken in his heart, for many years before that – perhaps even for most of the eighty years which we have come here in joy and thanksgiving to celebrate. We are celebrating today Cardinal Connell's years as a teacher, in philosophy, in theology and in the larger sense of participant in the church's magisterium.

To begin with, we will focus our attention on philosophy, in the university context, in which Cardinal Connell spent the first thirty-five years of his teaching service. They were thirty-five years of high achievement, measured not only in terms of scholarly publications and academic performance, but also in terms of the inspiration and encouragement and all kinds of scholarly support, which he gave so generously, both to his students and to his colleagues. Your Eminence, I am personally very happy to have this opportunity today to acknowledge my own debt of gratitude to you.

I did not have the privilege of being a student of Cardinal – Professor – Connell, but I was a faculty colleague, albeit in a different discipline. Professor Connell, as he then was, and I served together as members of a faculty of arts committee for the reform of the bachelor of arts degree, a committee, whose work, I remember, was not only time-consuming but also, as it sometimes appeared, time-locked as well. But Professor Connell's interventions, both there and at the faculty itself, were always a joy to listen to. They were full of insight, and delivered with precision and clarity.

In the university, Cardinal – Professor – Connell drew to himself friends from many different disciplines, but I think that it is noteworthy that among them were the musicians and the historians of music, for music has always been one of Cardinal Connell's great loves. In fact – I don't know how secret this is – Cardinal Connell is a secret player of the violin. And he shares this love of making music with another great churchman, one who received him in audience this morning, His Holiness Pope Benedict XVI.

We begin this happy and joyful day in celebration of Cardinal Connell's proximate eightieth birthday, by turning to that area of study which was his in the university – metaphysics. Our first speaker is Dr Fran O'Rourke, senior lecturer in the school of philosophy at University College Dublin. Dr O'Rourke is a graduate in philosophy and German of the National University of Ireland, Galway. Like Cardinal Connell, he completed his doctoral studies at the University of Louvain/Leuven, where he wrote his dissertation on Pseudo-Dionysius and Aquinas. Dr O'Rourke joined the staff of Cardinal Connell's department as a junior lecturer in 1980. He has published on a wide range of themes in metaphysics.

In 1992, Dr O'Rourke was the editor of a Festschrift in honour of the then Archbishop Desmond Connell, to mark his sixty-fifth birthday. In his preface to that volume, Dr O'Rourke described a Festschrift as a 'celebratory and collective gift, to honour a colleague in a special way.' I now have much pleasure in calling upon Dr O'Rourke to begin today's collective celebration in honour of His Eminence Desmond Cardinal Connell by delivering his paper on 'The beautiful dangers of being'.

Beautiful dangers of being[1]

FRAN O'ROURKE

Plato reveals optimistic realism in his endorsement of the ancient saying 'Beautiful things are difficult.'[2] On the challenge of affirming the soul's immortality, he is equally daring: 'Beautiful is the danger.'[3] Jacques Maritain has remarked: 'Difficult are the beautiful things: they summon us to beautiful dangers.' He continues: 'Plato has told us that beautiful things are difficult, but that we must not avoid the beautiful dangers. The human species would be placed in peril, and soon in despair, if it shed the beautiful dangers of intelligence and reason.'[4] Philosophy is a bold response to our need to make sense of the world. Aristotle also recognised the challenge and beauty of the task, praising Thales and Anaxagoras who ignored human interests and sought instead the 'extraordinary, wonderful, difficult and divine'.[5]

The difficulties of reason are many: philosophy, and metaphysics in particular, is a risky business! Immanuel Kant famously referred to the latter as 'a dark ocean, without shores or lighthouse'.[6] To philosophise is to

---

1 I am grateful to Gerard Casey, Brendan Purcell, and Patrick Sammon for many helpful suggestions and stylistic improvements.

2 *Republic* 435c: χαλεπὰ τὰ καλά.   3 *Phaedo* 114d: καλὸς γὰρ ὁ κίνδυνος.

4 Jacques Maritain, *Oeuvres Complètes* XI (Fribourg, 1991), p. 15: 'Platon nous a dit que les choses belles sont difficiles, et que nous ne devons pas esquiver les beaux dangers. L'espèce humaine serait mise en peril, et serait bientôt au désespoir, si elle se dérobait aux beaux dangers de l'intelligence et de la raison.'

5 *Nicomachean Ethics* 6, 7, 1141b6–8: περιττὰ μὲν καὶ θαυμαστὰ καὶ χαλεπὰ καὶ δαιμόνια.

6 From the Preface to 'Der einzig mögliche Beweisgrund zu einer Demonstration des Daseins Gottes' (1763): 'Zu diesem Zwecke aber zu gelangen muß man sich auf den bodenlosen Abgrund der Metaphysik wagen. Ein finsterer Ocean ohne Ufer und ohne Leuchtthürme, wo man es wie der Seefahrer auf einem unbeschifften Meere anfangen muß, welcher, so bald er irgendwo Land betritt, seine Fahrt prüft und untersucht, ob nicht etwa unbemerkte Seeströme seinen Lauf verwirrt haben, aller Behutsamkeit ungeachtet, die die Kunst zu schiffen nur immer gebieten mag' (AA II, 55–56). See 'The only possible argument in support of a demonstration of the existence of God', in

venture forth upon the fathomless and boundless ocean of existence itself. To be or not to be? That *is* the ultimate question. Friedrich Schelling remarked: 'If I go to the limits of all thought, I must recognise it as possible that there were nothing at all. The final question is always, "Why is there anything at all, why is there not nothing?"'[7] Martin Heidegger declares: 'Man alone of all beings, summoned by the voice of Being, experiences the wonder of all wonders: that beings are.'[8]

It has been correctly stated that the problems most difficult to solve are those that do not exist. Descartes posed such a problem when he thought it necessary to prove both his own existence, and that of the world. Maritain has remarked that Descartes, with his clear and distinct ideas, divorced intelligence from mystery.[9] While ancient philosophy was grounded upon the wonder of reality, modern philosophy is rooted in the scepticism of human doubt.[10] Being, however, is at once mysterious and intelligible. It has its own evidence, and the first evidence is that things are. At each moment we experience, in the words of the Northern Irish poet, Louis MacNeice, 'The blessedness of fact / Which lives in the dancing atom and the breathing trees'.[11] The fully real is the fully knowable, even while it remains for us unknown.[12] Being is the aim and object of all endeavour, the

Immanuel Kant, *Works: Theoretical Philosophy, 1755–1770*, ed. and trans. David Walford & Ralf Meerbote (Cambridge, 1992), p. III.

7 Friedrich Schelling, *Philosophie der Offenbarung* I (Darmstadt, 1955), p. 242: '[W]enn ich bis an die Grenze alles Denkens gehen will, so muß ich ja auch als möglich anerkennen, daß überall nichts wäre. Die letzte Frage ist immer: warum ist überhaupt etwas, warum ist nicht nichts?' See also Siger of Brabant, *Quaestiones in IV Metaph.*, ed. W. Dunphy (Louvain-la-Neuve, 1981), pp 169f: 'Si enim quaeratur quare est magis aliquid in rerum natura quam nihil'.

8 Martin Heidegger, *Was ist Metaphysik?* (Frankfurt am Main, 1969), pp 46f.

9 Jacques Maritain, *Creative intuition in art and poetry* (New York, 1960), p. 162.

10 See Alfred North Whitehead, *Science and the modern world* (London, 1985), p. 174: 'The ancient world takes its stand upon the drama of the Universe, the modern world upon the inward drama of the Soul.' Also Stephen R.L. Clark, *Aristotle's man: speculations upon Aristotelian anthropology* (Oxford, 1983), p. 83: 'It does not seem to have occurred to Aristotle seriously to doubt common reality: the doubt is perhaps pathological.'

11 Louis MacNeice, 'Ode' in *Collected Poems* (London, 1979), p. 55.

12 Martin Heidegger remarks: 'Ordinary thinking stops with the not-knowing of what is still knowable. The thinker's essential knowledge begins with the knowing of the

goal of mind and will. Being is the ubiquitous element of the human spirit: the ebb and flow of all we do, the buoyancy and ballast of what we know, the keel on which rests each intellectual advance. It is the anchor of every affirmation, the north which guides our quest – equally each point which encompasses the boundless sphere both of what we know and what yet remains uncharted.

Philosophy is infused from the start and sustained throughout by a sense of marvel before the mystery of reality. This is the well-spring of philosophy, characterised by an openness to the totality, both known and mysterious. It is inspired by the desire to comprehend – not necessarily to explain but to contemplate and ponder, to accept and appreciate. Philosophy itself begins in wonder and proceeds by reflective inquiry. This is well captured in the Irish saying: *Osclaíonn ceist ceist eile, doras feasa fiafrú*: 'Every question reveals another; enquiry is the portal of wisdom.'[13]

The questions of philosophy bear upon all the variety of human experience. One explanation of the word 'mystery' refers it to μύω, 'to close one eyes'. But as one writer suggests: 'The first step in philosophy is not a step; the first step is to open your eyes. Not until he has looked round him, and with more than a little astonishment, in the actual world, not until he has in some measure become "a spectator of all time and all existence", has any

---

unknowable. The scientist questions in order to reach serviceable answers. The thinker questions in order to ground the *questionability* of beings as a whole. The scientist always moves on the foundation of what has already been decided: that there is nature, that there is history, that there is art, that all of these can be made the object of observation. There is no such thing for the thinker. He stands within the decision of what there is at all and what beings are,' *Nietzsche* I (Pfullingen, 1961), p. 477. These lines are taken from the partial translation by Joan Stambaugh included in *Nietzsche: a collection of critical essays*, ed. Robert Solomon (New York, 1973), p. 110, rather than the complete translation of Heidegger's *Nietzsche*.

13   The complete quatrain, attributed to Gofraidh Fionn O Dálaigh, an eminent Munster poet of the second part of the fourteenth century, is as follows: 'To be inquisitive is to be knowledgeable; clever is the much-questioning poet: he detects the light through the obscurity; the door of wisdom is inquiry' (*Madh fiafruightheach, budh feasach; / glic an éigse ilcheasach, /solus na ceasa ad-chluinidh, / dorus feasa fiafruighidh*). See Thomas F. O'Rahilly in *Dánfhocail: Irish epigrams in verse* (Dublin, 1921), p. 13. I am grateful to Liam P. Ó Murchú for his excellent translation of these lines.

man a standing in the realm of thought.'[14] The Irish Nobel Prize winner, Seamus Heaney, has expressed the poet's realm in similar terms: 'I spend a lot of time just standing, looking, gazing with eyes and ears open. The inner place of your first being is a large solitary gaze out on the world.'[15] To be human is to inhabit a region bound by horizons not yet disclosed. Man lives at the frontier of the unknown; a frontier at every moment traversed, but over which he has little control. In his present condition man is a traveller or *viator* on an odyssey through reality; he is both player and spectator in the vast 'unfurling of entity'.[16] Knowledge and goodness are not given completely or all at once; human existence is achieved at the steady, inexorable pace of time; one of the earliest pronouncements of western philosophy is that nature likes to hide.[17] Our universe, however, is not an alien place; there is familiarity and ease in our engagement with the unknown. Uncertainty and expectancy about the future provide a hope and joy which are characteristically human; life would be monotonous if its every aspect were predictable. The world would hold little interest if it were comprehended by our limited minds.

Since uncertainty and an absence of complete knowledge are integral to human life, it is not surprising that 'unknowing' should characterise the greatest mystery in which we are ourselves involved. For each individual the enigma of existence has the character of a personal mystery. The mystery of being is the question of personal destiny in its ultimate context. All beings share in this mystery (*omnia exeunt in mysterium*) but it has special significance for man. Each person in the search for wisdom seeks his intimate identity, an identity which is inseparable from the fundamental mystery of the entire universe. Each being, no matter how humble, harbours the infinite wonder of being. To ask why anything exists, or why all things exist, is equally – and more significantly – to ask why I exist.

---

14   W. Macneile Dixon, *The human situation* (London, 1958), p. 211. The reference is to Plato, *Republic* 486a.

15   See Louise Johncox, 'Trip to the top', *The Times*, 28 Oct. 1995.

16   See Louis MacNeice, 'Plain speaking' in *Collected Poems*, p. 187.

17   Heraclitus, Fragment 123: φύσις κρύπτεσθαι φιλεῖ, in Hermann Diels & Walter Kranz, *Die Fragmente der Vorsokratiker* I (Berlin, 1961), p. 178.

Martin Heidegger perceptively remarks that there are two characteristics of metaphysical questioning: 'Firstly, every metaphysical question always covers the whole range of metaphysical problems. In every case it is itself the whole. Secondly, every metaphysical question can only be put in such a way that the questioner as such is by his very questioning involved in the question.'[18]

The question of Being is the most significant to which the mind can rise in speculation, the most profound facing each one in the challenge of personal destiny. Implicitly at least, existence must be the theme of all philosophy. Individual questions – those concerning man and the meaning of life, the existence of God, that of morality and the problem of knowledge – can be answered only in the light of a comprehensive philosophy of Being. The question of Being is in itself most natural and necessary; it is commensurate with the mystery of our own existence. The natural exigence of personal responsibility – the meaning we must find in, or confer upon, our lives – is none other than the question of Being, intensified in the beings which we ourselves are and experience most distinctively. For philosophy the question of being is the most universal and fundamental, for the philosopher it is the most personal.

The question of being brings with it the fascinating danger that we become unsettled; one might recall the words of Malebranche: 'I will not bring you into a strange land, but show perhaps that you are a stranger in your own country.'[19] Josef Pieper points out that to philosophise means to withdraw, not from the things of daily life, but from our habitual attitude towards them.[20] The unsettling aspect of the question is that we cannot place ourselves outside existence, and so delineate it as a precise question. Being is the source of all intelligibility, yet surpasses everything we under-

18   Martin Heidegger, *Was ist Metaphysik?* (Frankfurt am Main, 1969), p. 24.

19   Nicolas Malebranche, *Oeuvres complètes* 12, ed. A. Robinet (Paris, 1965), p. 30: 'Non, je ne vous conduirai point dans une terre étrangere: mais je vous apprendrai peut-être que vous êtes étranger vous-même dans vôtre propre païs.'

20   Josef Pieper, *Leisure the basis of culture* (London, 1952), p. 129. See Paul Valéry: 'Toute vue des choses qui n'est pas étrange est fausse. Si quelque chose est *réelle*, elle ne peut que perdre de sa réalité en devenant familière. Méditer en philosophe, c'est revenir du familier à l'étrange, et dans l'étrange affronter le réel': *Oeuvres* II (Paris, 1960), p. 501.

stand. To ask why anything exists is to place oneself in question; it is to experience the strange wonder that anything at all should be. Coleridge expresses it well:

> Hast thou ever raised thy mind to the consideration of EXISTENCE, in and by itself, as the mere act of existing? Hast thou ever said to thyself thoughtfully, IT IS! heedless in that moment whether it were a man before thee, or a flower, or a grain of sand? Without reference, in short, to this or that particular mode or form of existence? If thou hast indeed attained to this, thou wilt have felt the presence of a mystery, which must have fixed thy spirit in awe and wonder. The very words, There is nothing! or, There was a time, when there was nothing! are self-contradictory. There is that within us which repels the proposition with as full and instantaneous light, as if it bore evidence against the fact in the right of its own eternity. Not TO BE, then, is impossible: TO BE, incomprehensible. If thou hast mastered this intuition of absolute existence, thou wilt have learnt likewise that it was this, and no other, which in the earlier ages seized the nobler minds, the elect among men, with a sort of sacred horror.[21]

The poet asks us to consider existence 'without reference to this or that particular mode or form of existence'. This may be expressed in the following methodic principle: 'Being cannot be identified with any of its modes.' But what is existence apart from its modes – the things that are? Precisely this is what Martin Heidegger refers to as the 'ontological difference': the distinction between *Being*, and *that-which-is*.

Saint Bonaventure refers to the same difference in a striking analogy: 'Just as the eye, intent on the various differences of colour, does not see the light through which it sees other things, or if it does see, does not notice it, so our mind's eye, intent on particular and universal beings (*entia*), does not notice Being itself (*ipsum esse*) which is beyond all categories, even though it comes first to the mind, and through it, all other things.'[22] He

21   S.T. Coleridge, *Collected Works*, 4: *The Friend* I, ed. Barbara E. Rooke (London, 1993), p. 514. Emphasis in original.

22   Saint Bonaventure, *Itinerarium mentis in Deum* V, 4: *Works of Saint Bonaventure* II,

quotes Aristotle: 'As the eyes of bats are to the light of day, so is the intellect of our soul towards the things which by nature are most manifest of all.'[23] Most apparent of all is the very Being of beings, and yet faced with the mystery of Being we approach the border between light and dark. We are confronted by the undefined and indefinite; we experience a metaphysical vertigo.

This is the ultimate marvel of existence: we cannot pin it down, or confine it to any concept or category. This is what philosophers mean whey they say that being is a 'transcendental' concept; it surpasses and embraces all divisions among beings. Some even dispute that there is a concept of being at all. It cannot be coralled within confining boundaries; I have been told that the Arabic word for 'concept' is related to the term for the pen used to fence in camels. Existence cannot be 'cabin'd, cribb'd, confined, bound in'. Being may not be reduced to any particular kind, determination, or mode of being. All forms of *a priori* reduction are unwarranted. There could be other worlds of which we are unaware, 'parallel universes' or modes of existence which surpass our human measure. In its intrinsic meaning, being has no limitations. It is boundless in its connotation. It is an unwarranted assumption, therefore, that being is only the physical, just as it is unwarranted to believe that all that exists is either the mental or rational. Language is often misleading. 'To be *material*' is to *be*; 'to be *ideal*' is to *be*; 'to be *mental*' is to *be*. We cannot, however, invert these statements and conclude that 'to be' is simply 'to be *material*', or that 'to be' is nothing more than 'to be *ideal*' and so forth. Existence cannot be reduced to any one particular manner of being, or equated with any single determination. This is the 'ontological difference': the surplus and excess of *Being* beyond *that-which-is*.[24]

trans. Philotheus Boehner (New York, 1956), pp 82f: 'Sed sicut oculus intentus in varias colorum differentias lucem, per quam videt cetera, non videt, et si videt, non advertit; sic oculus mentis nostrae, intentus in entia particularia et universalia, ipsum esse extra omne genus, licet primo occurrat menti, et per ipsum alia, tamen non advertit.'

23   *Metaphysics* 2, 1, 993a10–12.
24   H.G. Wells refers to 'that ineluctable marginal inexactitude which is the most mysterious inmost quality of Being.' See *A modern utopia* (Lincoln, NA, 1967), pp 20f.

Μελέτα τὸ πᾶν: 'Look to the whole,' was the counsel of Periander, one of the Seven Sages. A seductive danger when viewing existence as a whole, and especially human nature, is to interpret the totality exclusively in terms of its parts: to reduce reality to a single aspect, or identify it with one of its limited manifestations. I will refer to two divergent extremes arising from this temptation: firstly and briefly, that of naturalistic materialism; secondly that of Platonic spiritualism. I will comment finally on man's precarious situation as he straddles the domains of matter and spirit, and the consequent need for an all-inclusive approach which embraces the mysterious via the intelligible, thus discerning the infinite origin of his identity.

The most obvious pitfall is to equate reality with the natural world, with what we physically touch and see here and now, and to say: 'This is all there is.' Such is the position of materialism, which denies all metaphysical reality beyond the tangible: the world that we see is sufficient in itself; nothing more is needed. In tandem with this danger is the temptation to reduce man to his material or biological nature. This temptation has accelerated in recent times with the altogether justified, but sometimes exaggerated, appeal of the theory of evolution and the marvellous successes of molecular biology. The discovery that man's DNA is 98 per cent identical with that of the chimpanzee has led some to assume that they are essentially the same. This is to overlook their radically different behaviour and the vastly distinct worlds that they inhabit. Metaphorically each animal resembles the snail: confined within its habitat, it cannot step outside, to reflect upon its universe or freely shape its destiny.

It is particularly ironic that, despite the diversity of life forms – estimated at between fourteen and thirty million – most biochemical and genetic generalisations are derived from just three organisms: the rat, the fruit fly and the common gut bug (*escherichia coli*) which, like the fast-breeding fruit fly (*drosophila*), has the advantage that it replicates and mutates rapidly, thus allowing scientists to accelerate the accumulation of data from which to extrapolate the patterns of evolution.[25] As for crass

25   See Steven Rose, *Lifelines: biology, freedom, determinism* (London, 1998), pp 2, 4.

materialistic reductionism, Herbert Joseph Muller remarks: 'To say that a man is made up of certain chemical elements is a satisfying description only for those who intend to use him as a fertilizer.'[26]

For the metaphysician, needless to say, there is more to the world than meets the eye. An enduring image for the 'step beyond' the given world, which marks the impetus and dynamism of metaphysics, is the ascent from Plato's cave; out of, and beyond, the sub-intelligible caverns of the imagination. A modern equivalent of Plato's shadow world is that of television. *Homo sapiens* has become *homo 'zapiens'*! Plato's challenge remains: to step beyond the world of the inauthentic and transitory to the plane of the enduring and the abiding. The soul must turn from darkness to light and ascend to real being – for Plato the true task of philosophy.

Jacques Maritain extolled what he considered the very poetry of Plato's thought. Plato's phrase, 'music' of the spirit, conveyed for him the comprehensive universality of philosophy itself. He lauded Plato's emphasis on the individual, personal, nature of the philosophic quest: 'I am inclined, now more than ever', he wrote, 'to think with Plato . . . that the most important thing for a philosopher is to "turn toward the internal city he bears within himself".'[27] In contrast to science, which is detached from the inquirer, wisdom functions in unity with the personal roots of the thinking human subject, in unity with the whole man. According to Plato, we must philosophise 'with the entire soul'; the entire being of the wise man is engaged in the work of wisdom.

While stressing that he is not a Platonist, Maritain refers to the 'natural Platonism of the human mind', namely that 'our mind is naturally drawn to eternal truths and transcendent values.'[28] Man, in the words of Plato's *Timaeus*, is 'a plant not of an earthly but of a heavenly growth'.[29] Plato has, in the words of Pseudo-Justin, 'the air of one who has descended from

26   Herbert J. Muller, *Science and criticism: the humanistic tradition in contemporary thought* (New Haven, 1943), p. 107.

27   *The social and political philosophy of Jacques Maritain*, ed. J.W. Evans & L.R. Ward (London, 1956), p. 14. See *Republic* 591e.

28   *Social and political philosophy*, p. 281.

29   *Timaeus* 90a: φυτὸν οὐκ ἔγγειον, ἀλλ᾽ οὐράνιον.

above, who has accurately ascertained and seen all that is in heaven'.[30] Plato's devotion to the eternal and transcendent is illustrated in Raphael's depiction of the School of Athens, and expressed by Goethe as follows: 'Plato seems to behave as a spirit descended from heaven, who has chosen to dwell a space on earth. He hardly attempts to know this world. He has already formed an idea of it, and his chief desire is to communicate to mankind, which stands in such need of them, the truths which he has brought with him and delights to impart. If he penetrates to the depths of things, it is to fill them with his own soul, not to analyse them. Without intermission and with the burning ardour of his spirit, he aspires to rise and regain the heavenly abode from which he came down. The aim of all his discourse is to awaken in his hearers the notion of a single eternal being, of the good, of truth, of beauty. His method and words seem to melt, to dissolve into vapour, whatever scientific facts he has managed to borrow from the earth.'[31]

But herein, precisely, lies the peril. This natural élan towards eternal truth and transcendent value, the 'natural Platonism of the mind', brings with it the beautiful danger of metaphysical hubris, the gnostic temptation to overstep its powers. The desire and capacity to know outstretch the means and method which are our measure. Intelligence is destined for being, but it is our lot to search it out in corruptible things. In seeking Being it finds only the elusive becoming of sensible flux in individual and changing reality. Deceived and scandalised, Plato turns his gaze to a separate world of essences, a spectral world; he sketches a metaphysic of the *extra-real*, conceived after the manner of mathematics, a metaphysical mirage, while the sensible world is delivered over to illusion and opinion. Plato, as Kant so pictorially remarked, believed the soul would discover truth more easily if it were liberated from the body: 'The light dove, cleaving the air in her free flight and feeling its resistance, might imagine that it would ascend yet more easily in airless space. It was thus that Plato

30   See Christoph Riedweg (ed.), *Ps.-Justin (Markell von Ankara?), Ad Graecos de vera religione (bisher 'Cohortatio ad Graecos')* (Basel, 1994), 5, 2.
31   J.W. Goethe, *Naturwissenschaftliche Schriften* 3 (Weimar, 1893), p. 141, trans. Jacques Maritain, *An introduction to philosophy* (London, 1947), p. 68, n. 1.

left the world of the senses, and ventured beyond it upon the wings of ideas into the empty void of pure understanding. He did not observe that with all his efforts he made no advance, meeting no resistance against which to apply his powers, and so set his understanding in motion.'[32]

Metaphysics lies midway between the spiritual and the sensible. Aristotle – Plato's pupil, but more importantly a disciple of nature – forged a surer path; he restored the integrity of sensible things, an approach well expressed by the poet MacNeice:

> Aristotle was better who watched the insect breed,
> The natural world develop,
> Stressing the function, scrapping the Form in Itself,
> Taking the horse from the shelf and letting it gallop.[33]

Plato's error derives from his method. Determined to ground the scientific character of knowledge, he misinterpreted the process of cognition and mistook in turn the nature of the knower. Plato's spiritualism, like that of Descartes, scorns the body and the sense faculties; it despises empirical reality. His error was to presume there is a royal road to metaphysical truth, a revelation like that of the goddess to Parmenides, bestowed on one who is transported by divine messengers beyond the ways of men. Sadly, there is no high road to the transcendent for the metaphysician; metaphysics is hard work!

Both Aristotle and Aquinas reject Plato's deprecation of sensible being – for them the sense world is the natural and proper domain of our first encounter with the actuality of existence, what really is and can be really known. They reject his ideal reality, subsisting in itself with the selfsame characteristics which it enjoys in thought – abstract, universal, unique, eternal, immaterial. Plato, like many others, fell victim to another danger in defining being. Just as we may not identify existence with any of its modes, we may not confuse *what* we know with the *way* in which we know it. From this confusion there follows yet a third reductionist pitfall, when

32   Immanuel Kant, *Critique of Pure Reason*, trans. Norman Kemp Smith (London, 1985), p. 47.
33   Louis MacNeice, 'Autumn journal' in *Collected Poems*, p. 124.

method predetermines the nature of what is investigated. Plato and the materialist alike are victims of their respective methods: if all you have is a hammer, everything ends up looking like a nail.

Aristotle and Aquinas reject the unnatural dualism of Plato, his metaphysical and epistemological apartheid. Man is for Aristotle, and more clearly for Aquinas, a unity of body and soul, matter and spirit. He constitutes, Aquinas notes, a horizon, inhabiting the frontier between spiritual and bodily reality: he is the medium between two worlds, partaking both of spiritual and bodily goodnesses.[34] The human soul resides on the boundary of the temporal and the eternal, the material and spiritual, beyond time and beneath eternity.[35] A spiritual substance, it is the form of the human body. This is the most remarkable instance of 'the wonderful connection of things' (*mirabilis rerum connexio*),[36] whereby divine wisdom joins the lowest of the superior grade to what is highest within the inferior. Man is a part of nature but forms also a nature apart; he is inserted within the physical world but also stands beyond it.

Man can be described moreover as a microcosm, a world in miniature, in two senses. Firstly, through the intentional openness of spirit, he mirrors in a truly wonderful and mysterious manner within his consciousness the totality of the universe. Secondly, he embodies within himself the diverse levels of being. Pascal sums up well our cognitive relation to the world: 'By space the universe contains me as a speck; by thinking I contain it.'[37] (This is one of the clearest indications of man's spiritual nature: how could an infinitesimal portion of matter embrace within itself the entire universe?)

34   *In III Sententias*, Prol.: 'Homo enim est quasi horizon et confinium spiritualis et corporalis naturae, ut quasi medium inter utrasque, utrasque bonitates participet et corporales et spirituales.'

35   *In de causis* 9: 'Anima est in horizonte aeternitatis et temporis existens infra aeternitatem et supra tempus.'

36   *Contra gentiles* 2, 68.

37   *Pensées*, no. 348: 'Ce n'est point de l'espace que je dois chercher ma dignité, mais c'est du règlement de ma pensée. Je n'aurai pas davantage en possédant des terres: par l'espace, l'univers me comprend et m'engloutit comme un point; par la pensée, je le comprends': *Oeuvres de Blaise Pascal*, 13; *Pensées* II, ed. Léon Brunschvicg (Paris, 1904; repr. Liechtenstein, 1976), p. 263.

Quoting Aristotle, that the soul is 'in some manner, all things',[38] since its nature is to know all things, Aquinas states: 'it is possible for the perfection of the entire universe to exist in one thing.'[39] Through his spiritual nature, man has a relation to all of reality. The Arabic thinker Avicenna declares that the ultimate perfection which the soul can attain is to have delineated in it the entire order and causes of the universe. Aquinas relates this to man's ultimate end, which is the vision of God; on the horizon of material and spiritual, man receives all things, sensible and spiritual. 'The senses receive the species of all sensible things, the intellect those of intelligible things; thus through sense and intellect the soul of man is in some way all things. In this manner those endowed with knowledge approach in similarity to God, in whom, according to Dionysius, all things preexist.'[40]

But man's perfection is not only spiritual, but also ontological. The perfections of all things are not just reflected in him cognitively, but are exemplified existentially in his nature. Within himself he discerns the scale and diversity of being. All levels of reality are unified within his complex singularity: material, vegetable, animal, spiritual. Within himself he can sound the depths and densities of the real. In the self are harmonized the many levels of reality – from material to spiritual, from the individual to the universal. Immersed within the material world, he feels the weight of his sensible nature, but through his spiritual activity he assumes a personal freedom within the universe. Within ourselves we acutely experience the mystery of existence. It is both mystical and visceral: we feel it in the beating pulse of pleasure and pain, in the refreshing vigour of physical exertion, in the throes of anguish and the frisson of joy, in the élan of love which quickens in the presence of the beloved. To modify a phrase from Gerard Manley Hopkins, I savour existence best at the tankard of the self: 'I find myself both as a man and as myself something more determined and distinctive, at pitch more distinctive and higher pitched than anything else I see.'[41] Within himself man experiences most intensely the riches of being.

38   *De anima* 3, 8, 431b21.
39   *De veritate* 2, 2.
40   *Summa theologiae* I, 80.
41   G.M. Hopkins, *Poems and prose* (London, 1953), p. 145.

Man was created, Aquinas notes, that the universe might be complete; all of nature tends toward the perfection of man. It is not man, needless to say, but God who gives the world its meaning. Man's presence, however, gives an intelligible visibility the world would otherwise lack. He is, as it were, the eye of the universe, through which the world becomes visible to itself. Perhaps W.B. Yeats had something like this in mind when he declared: 'We can make our minds so like still water that beings gather about us that they may see, it may be, their own images, and so live for a moment with a clearer, perhaps even with a fiercer life because of our quiet.'[42] Man gives to the world a meaning it would not have except in his sight.

Just as all the existential riches of the world flow from the intensive, emergent, act of existence, the self is the mysterious and elusive depth from which emerge all our activities: they proceed from the individual act of personal being. Knowledge of the self is the most revealing disclosure of reality to which we have access: not a disembodied self but a personal 'I' which stands forth from the material universe but which does not abandon it, which transcends the dimensions of time and space but never escapes them. Incorporating all levels of existing perfection, man recognises himself to be what is most perfect in the natural universe. Man is not only what he knows best, but also the best of what he knows. He is what is most perfect within his own experience. But he feels most acutely also his onto-logical *in-difference*: I am the source neither of myself nor of the world. Nothing in my nature demands that I should by any necessity exist rather than not. Hopkins remarks: 'When I ask where does this throng and stack of being, so rich, so distinctive, so important, come from, nothing I see can answer me.'[43] Within ourselves we perceive most sharply the existential indigence or ontological indifference of the universe. I find myself at the apex of the visible universe, yet know that I am the origin neither of myself nor of the world.

Although the self is both what we know best, and the best of what we

42   W.B. Yeats, *The Celtic twilight* (Gerrards Cross, Bucks., 1981), p. 100.
43   G.M. Hopkins, *Poems and prose*, p. 145.

know, each person still remains a mystery to himself. Heraclitus rightly
declares: 'You could not in your going find the ends of the soul, though you
travelled the whole way: so deep is its Logos.'[44] The self is the place in the
universe where we best read the signature of the creator. In vain could we
derive the wonder of life from the mechanical processes of the inorganic
world: nor can the cognitive and volitional life of the soul, with its outward
openness upon universal being and inward depths of reflective selfhood, be
reduced to the biological processes of animal operations. What is greater
cannot proceed from the lesser; just as it is impossible for being to spring
from non-being. To hold that all the marvels of the human world are no
more than the progeny of lifeless matter is to strain credulity.

The spirit has an infinite capacity which remains unfulfilled by what is
finite. Man has an endless requirement for truth and goodness, a demand
which characterizes both intellect and will. He has need of total happiness:
to know and enjoy an unlimited good. Disclosing the infinite origin of the
universe man discovers himself – in knowing the fullness of Being. Only in
God will he find, in Aquinas' words, 'the loveliness of spring, the brightness
of summer, the abundance of autumn and the repose of winter'.[45]

Man's crowning intellectual attainment is to discern his identity as
image of the infinite maker. The greatest difficulty in affirming the reality
of God lies in the greatness of its truth. The great unknown is an unknown
greatness. The existence of God is a truth too difficult for the human mind
to accommodate: that there should exist a person, infinite in being and
unceasing in love, whose nature it is simply to be – to be absolutely – such
that it is impossible for him not to exist; whose goodness is so generous as
to generate the entire universe. It is almost natural for our intellect to baulk
before a truth so wonderful and sublime, since it is at ease only with what it
can calculate and control. The alternative to mystery, however, is absurdity
or contradiction: to claim that the world, which is insufficient in each of its
aspects, is in need of nothing beyond itself. In the words of one author: 'By

44 Fragment 45: ψυχῆς πείρατα ἰὼν οὐκ ἂν ἐξεύροιο, πᾶσαν ἐπιπορευόμενος ὁδόν· οὕτω
βαθὺν λόγον ἔχει: Diels & Kranz, *Die Fragmente der Vorsokratiker* I, p. 161.

45 *Opuscula theologica* 2: 'amoenitas vernalis, luciditas aestivalis, ubertas autumnalis, et
requies hiemalis'.

accepting the freedom of the first cause, we make the contradiction disappear, but in its stead we find an ineffable and inscrutable mystery. Yet despite its obscurity this mystery is the light in which the whole of all finite beings, the world, becomes to some extent intelligible.'[46]

Democritus, the founder of atomic theory, declared: 'In reality we know nothing, for truth is in the depths.'[47] There is a dissymmetry between our knowledge and ultimate intelligibility. The clarity of human cognition is at odds with the luminosity proper to existence. Considered in themselves, in respect of their origin, creatures are shadow and darkness, compared to God who is light itself. As the bat is blinded by the sun, human vision is overpowered by the excessive intelligibility of divine being. Our knowledge of God is eclipsed by divine brightness and seems obscure. But only from darkness can light be seen; whoever digs deep enough will see the stars in daylight. Divine light bathes creation throughout its vast circumference in a mysterious radiance, but remains itself obscure: what to us seems darkness is the infinity of light. God remains hidden, that he can be known as God. W.B. Yeats recognised the appropriate response:

> God loves dim ways of glint and gleam;
> To please him well my verse must be
> A dyed and figured mystery;
> Thought hid in thought, dream hid in dream.[48]

The question of being, which awakens in wonder at the least significant reality, is refined and purified, restored to its source, when we answer that it is a gratuitous gift from the unlimited Good. With this response the question is not simply answered; it has been enlarged and given an infinite dimension. It has become absorbed into mystery and no longer needs an

46 John A. Peters, *Metaphysics: a systematic survey* (Pittsburgh, 1963), p. 466, n. 157.
47 Fragment 117: ἐτεῆι δὲ οὐδὲν ἴδμεν· ἐν βυθῶι γὰρ ἡ ἀλήθεια: Diels & Kranz, *Die Fragmente der Vorsokratiker* II (Berlin, 1960), p. 166.
48 Cited by Richard Ellmann in *The identity of Yeats* (London, 1968), p. 24. The first two lines vary slightly from the version printed in W.B. Yeats, *The early poetry* II, ed. George Bornstein (Ithaca, 1987), p. 489.

answer. There has occurred not only a change in the question but with it a change in the enquirer and in our relation to what is questioned: the mystery of infinite Being. We cannot now place the question before us, but stand within its immensity. Wonder at the first mystery of being gives way to a love of the absolute good which has given creation to us for the sake of our fulfilment. The appropriate thinking is now a thanking, the appropriate response is not of question but of gratitude. Coleridge expresses it well: 'In wonder all philosophy began; in wonder it ends: and admiration fills up the interspace. But the first wonder is the offspring of ignorance: the last is the parent of adoration.'[49]

The Italian philosopher Cornelio Fabro gave to one of his books the paradoxic title *Man and the risk of God*.[50] There are indeed risks attached to the affirmation of God, through the consequent and inevitable demands upon one's life and actions. As the protagonist in Robert Penn Warren's *All the king's men* remarks: 'God and Nothing have a lot in common. You look either one of Them straight in the eye for a second and the immediate effect on the human constitution is the same.'[51] Such an option bears upon the fundamental paths of human action, freedom and ultimate fulfilment. We explore them at our risk, but ignore them at our peril. The most beautiful 'danger' is to affirm one's indigence and total dependence upon the infinite, and to take the consequences freely to heart. Again Plato provides encouragement: 'The prize is beautiful and the hope is great.'[52]

49   S.T. Coleridge, *Aids to reflection*, ed. John Beer, *Collected Works*, 9 (London, 1993), p. 236.

50   Cornelio Fabro, *L'Uomo e il rischio di dio* (Roma, 1967).

51   Robert Penn Warren, *All the king's men* (New York, 1963), p. 139. See G.K. Chesterton, *Heretics*, (London, 1928), pp 58f: 'Until we realize that things might not be, we cannot realize that things are. Until we see the background of darkness we cannot admire the light as a single and created thing. As soon as we have seen that darkness, all light is lightning, sudden, blinding, and divine. Until we picture nonentity we underrate the victory of God, and can realize none of the trophies of His ancient war.'

52   *Phaedo* 114c: καλὸν γὰρ τὸ ἆθλον καὶ ἡ ἐλπὶς μεγάλη.

Return to wonder

LINDA ZAGZEBSKI

PHILOSOPHY BEGINS IN WONDER. What happens next? What a philosopher does next tells you everything about the radical divergence in philosophical traditions in the last four hundred years. Dr O'Rourke describes a path from wonder that I find edifying and compelling, but it is not the only possible path. An important feature of the wonder at Being so vividly captured in O'Rourke's paper is that it is not detached. We do not simply observe Being and notice how fascinating it is. Being is not separated from our own being, and it is not separated from value, so to wonder at Being is simultaneously to be enthralled by good, and it leads us to desire a view of our role in the world that satisfies desires other than the cognitive, other than the desire for truth. We want a role that connects us to Being, not just to the local modes of being that we encounter in the course of our short lifetimes. People who have this attitude towards Being have a religious temperament even if they do not practise a religion. This is the path taken not only by the world's great religions, but by most of the philosophies in the history of the world until recently.

What other path from wonder might one take? The rise of atheism in the modern era coincides with a different line of inquiry also driven by wonder, but it differs from the wonder described by Dr O'Rourke in two important ways. First, being and value are separated, so wonder at being has nothing to do with any particular attitude towards good and beauty. And second, wonder is not directed at one's own being. Being may be amazing, but one's own being is not. So the atheist naturalist at the beginning of the twenty-first century maintains that we have no reason to think that there is any connection between the fulfillment of the desire for truth and the desire for individual value or connectedness to the whole of being. When I wonder at being, I may not assume that I am important. I should try to figure out how the world is put together as best I can, and the best way to do that is to use the scientific method. If I am honest, I must admit that what I discover is that there is no special role in the universe for me. Religion is a 'consolation.' It is what keeps most people going, taking away the anxiety of being, but it has nothing to do with the way the world really is. Those with a more stalwart spirit do not need it.

I find it interesting that the person with this kind of sensibility does have a sense of connectedness, but it is only on the material level. If I have a religious temperament, I think that just as my body is part of a vast material world outside myself, my soul is part of a vast spiritual world outside myself. The naturalist has no trouble acknowledging the former; it is the latter he resists.

Let me compare two atheist naturalists, one of whom lacks the religious temperament, and one of whom clearly has it. The first is Richard Dawkins. When Dawkins accepted the Humanist of the Year award in 1996, he said in his speech that science itself satisfies religious sensibilities. Dawkins says:

> it's exactly this feeling of spine-shivering, breath-catching awe – almost worship – this flooding of the chest with ecstatic wonder, that modern science can provide. And it does so beyond the wildest dreams of saints and mystics. The fact that the supernatural has no place in our explanations, in our understanding of so much about the universe and life, doesn't diminish the awe. Quite the contrary. The merest glance through a microscope at the brain of an ant or through a telescope at a long-ago galaxy of a billion worlds is enough to render poky and parochial the very psalms of praise.

On Dawkins' account, the universe as described by physics is amazing, even awe-inspiring, but my place in it is not amazing; it is, in fact, trivial. Nothing in Dawkins' remarks express a sense of connectedness to Being or the good or even a desire for it. Like the majority of American philosophers, Dawkins lacks the religious temperament.

In contrast, the philosopher Thomas Nagel is an atheist naturalist who appreciates the religious temperament, and who has written a stunningly

forthright and astute description of why atheistic naturalism is so unsatis-
fying. For Nagel, religion is out, but he admits that secular philosophy is
having a very hard time finding something to put in its place. He says that
is because there is a human desire to participate in the universe, not just
exist in it. '[H]aving, amazingly, burst into existence, one is a representative
of existence itself – of the whole of it – not just because one is part of it but
because it is present to one's consciousness. In each of us, the universe has
come to consciousness, and therefore our existence is not merely our own.'

Nagel goes on to say that what he calls 'hardheaded atheism' simply
dismisses the issue raised by the person with a religious temperament. He
then considers three ways to satisfy the religious yearning while main-
taining atheism. One is humanism, the idea that the gap left by the loss of
religion is filled by ourselves as a species or as a community. The cosmic
ambitions of humanism are very limited and Nagel calls it 'too feeble an
answer'. The second is existentialist defiance according to which the
universe is pointless, but I find meaning in the refusal to accept it. This
answer has greater cosmic scope than humanism and Nagel considers it a
viable option. The third is non-reductive, teleological naturalism. Nothing
exists but the natural world, but biology does not reduce to physics,
consciousness does not reduce to physical processes, value does not reduce
to descriptions, and there are irreducible principles of organisation in the
world that govern temporally extended development, including evolu-
tionary processes, that are not merely mechanistic, but which are not
mentally caused. They are neither accidental nor caused by a divine being.
We are not accidents. We are part of something larger – nature itself.

I don't know if Nagel's hypothesis satisfies the religious sense of wonder
or even if the hypothesis makes sense. I mention it only because I think
Nagel is one of the few philosophers who understands how a religious
answer to the first question of philosophy – Why is there something rather
than nothing? – diverges from the answer of atheist naturalism. He does
not pretend that the atheist has better evidence for his world-view than the
theist. In fact, he denies that. He understands that how we understand
Being and our connection to it depends upon what question we are asking
about it and what it is in us that produces the question. Nagel is too smart

to say that the question that comes out of a religious temperament should be dismissed because he no doubt realises that we can say the same thing about the questions to which scientific answers are appropriate. In other words, if the natural desire for connectedness and purpose is not satisfiable, why think that the natural desire for truth about the physical universe is satisfiable? And conversely, if, as the naturalist assumes, the desire for truth is satisfiable, why not other natural desires as well?

Philosophy begins in wonder and different philosophical traditions diverge immediately. That is why it is so hard to talk across the boundaries of continental and analytic philosophy, religious philosophy and naturalism, and the many other divides within contemporary philosophy. To get to what we have in common sometimes means going all the way back to the beginning, to the wonder that brought us to philosophy in the first place.

A changing horizon

BISHOP BRIAN FARRELL

I WAS REALLY DELIGHTED when Monsignor Bergin invited me to chair this part of the Irish College's excellent initiative in honour of Cardinal Desmond Connell. There seems to be something profoundly un-Irish, or at least it's not something usual in Dublin, for a room of educated people to sit around saying nice things about someone. Already in the eighteenth century Samuel Johnson wrote: 'The Irish are not in a conspiracy to cheat the world by false representations of the merits of their countrymen. No, sir, the Irish are a fair people – they never speak well of one another.' But this afternoon's programme is such that there is no need to trot out any of the trivial pleasantries that we often do on such occasions. There is plenty of substance here to give us the deeper and more exact framework for our appreciation of the man and his achievements.

When I was growing up in the Dublin of the 1950s and very early 60s, the church loomed huge on my personal horizon and on every other horizon familiar to me at the time. Fortunately for me it was a positive presence: the church taught me that my life had meaning beyond myself. Later, I often described those years as having been lived in a veritable novitiate, an immense, public, communitarian, place in which every aspect of life, personal and social, was marked by spirituality, by sacramentality, by the mysterious presence of the divine behind every human experience.

There was an ordered certainty about things. The truths and values by which we lived – which were nurtured and reinforced by all kinds of motivations, convincing or not – stood out as fixed and solid signposts. You could hate them and reject them; you could rebel and refuse to live by them. But you still felt them there, staring at you and judging you, and always urging you to do the right thing. It was more or less the same all over Europe, whether Catholic Europe or Protestant Europe.

Today, my nieces and nephews – and their Irish and European peers –

live with very few certainties, and with little order in their lives. They all have jobs, and live comfortably. But they will admit that the society in which they live is not a reassuring place. It is conflictive and sometimes cruel. On their horizon the church is mostly absent. It serves at special moments, either as a backdrop and ceremonial to solemnise their marriages, if they marry; or to offer a temporary comfort at times of loss, through its funeral pageantry.

The change is extraordinarily deep and abiding. I believe it has less to do with tigers, Celtic or otherwise, and all to do with metaphysics, or rather the loss of metaphysics, as the ground on which to build the core ideas of a civilisation that has the human person and the common good at its heart. It is a matter of philosophical and theological anthropology: the crisis is about what it means to be human in today's 'brave new world.'

Cardinal Connell, much against his own deepest personal yearnings, I am convinced, has had to take a public role in this very difficult time of transition. I had never met him until he became archbishop of Dublin. Since then, I think I can say that we have had a genuine friendship. I like the definition of friendship which goes: 'A friend is one who understands our silence.' Important moments should be wrapped in a silent search for understanding. I am convinced that when historians gain some perspective on the cultural upheaval of recent decades, they will write much more positively about Cardinal Connell's response to it than they are likely to do today.

In 1907, Robert Hugh Benson wrote: 'It has been well observed that there is no such thing as an impartial historian. Every man who sets out to trace the development of life, whether in politics, religion, or art, is bound to do so with some theory in his mind . . . The historian, or the theologian, who is most nearly partial is not he who has no view, but he who is aware of other views, and can give them due consideration.' Your Eminence, the time for serene consideration will come.

At a symposium of the European bishops (October 1982) Pope John Paul II stated: 'The crisis of European culture is the crisis of christian culture . . . the drama of Europe does not only challenge Christianity and the church from without, as if it were some external difficulty or obstacle, but in some sense it is internal to Christianity and the church. We discover, perhaps with a sense of amazement, that the crises and temptations of European man and of Europe are crises and temptations of Christianity and the church in Europe.'

To help us enter a theological reflection on the reality of today's Europe, let me introduce Dr Brendán Leahy, professor of dogmatic theology at Maynooth. The Pontifical Council for promoting Christian Unity recently incurred a new debt with Brendán. This year in the week of prayer for Christian unity, people around the world have been using the texts prepared by an inter-church group in Ireland that Brendán brought together. The texts were then jointly published by our office and the World Council of Churches and they have been universally praised for their spiritual insight and ecumenical sensitivity, drawn from the lived-experience of Irish life.

The triune God's reply to Europe's contemporary cry

BREANDÁN LEAHY

LOOKING BACK OVER European history there have been various outcries of anguish on this continent: the cry of alarm that 'the world is ending' in the fifth century with the unprepared-for collapse of the western Roman Empire; the cry of defiance in the eighth century in the face of Arab invasion halted by Charles Martel in 732; the cries of anger and misunderstanding during the tragic split between the eastern and western sides of Christendom in the first centuries of the second millennium. And of course, the wounded cries of the sixteenth-century religious wars. More recently, the outcries of revulsion at the awful events of the twentieth-century world wars initiated in Europe continue to haunt.

There is, however, a contemporary cry in Europe that pierces in an altogether new way. It is a multi-toned cry of indifference towards, rejection of or simply perceived painful absence of God as a comprehensive horizon. This results in what the German theologian, Eugene Biser, calls a 'landscape of the cry' that can be seen not least in modern literature, philosophy, and psychology.[1] We could add that it is audible also in many modern socio-political developments.

This experience of a 'lack of God', 'missing but not missed', as has been said, is not always explicitly adverted to in the hearts and minds of contemporary European men and women. Our culture, as Heidegger puts it, is so poor and distracted from thinking that it no longer recognises the lack of God as lack.[2]

Of course, we cannot but acknowledge with gratitude the great strides

---

1 E. Beiser, *Glaubenswende: Eine Hoffnungsperspektive* (Freiburg, 1987), p. 113.
2 M. Heidegger, 'The Word of God "God is dead"' in *The question concerning technology and other essays*, trans. by W. Lovitt (London, 1977), pp 53–114.

forward that have marked recent centuries. Each of us benefits from them. And yet we know that, for many, a nihilism operates in the background of day-to-day choices, activities and interpretations of life. People live 'as if God did not exist'.

Existence has been reduced to fragments without an overall horizon; it is understood for the most part as consumption of products, the doing of tasks in a race guided by media sound bites. We have increasingly become trapped within a history closed in on itself with all kinds of results, not least the collapse of the foundations of ethics, new outbreaks of racial intolerance, a diminishing of social solidarity, and rampant features of a 'culture of death'. At times we feel there's a faceless, technocratic power that risks enveloping us. The film *The Matrix* placed this before us.

Nietzsche's words capture something of our current European socio-spiritual horizon: 'Has it not become colder? Is it not night and more night coming on all the time?'[3]

EUROPE – A CULTURE WITHOUT GOD?

In his work, *La troisième mort du Dieu*, André Glucksmann puts before us the phenomenon that God is dying. In Europe, indeed, he is already dead. Glucksmann then goes on to ask: Why Europe? Why only Europe, the only continent, in the whole world and in humanity's history to produce a civilisation without God?[4]

Theorists, of course, will debate the exact nature of the transformation of the European religious landscape. As the 1999 European Values Study noted, there is even a certain religious renewal in Europe with signs of a certain 'new visibility of religion in Europe'. Grace Davie notes this too but she describes it as a 'believing without belonging.' Lieven Boeve of Louvain summarises our situation in terms of 'post-secular':

---

3   F. Nietzsche, *The gay science*, Third Book, Aphorism 258, trans. W. Kaufmann (New York, 1974), p. 125.
4   A. Glucksmann, *La troisième mort du Dieu* (Paris, 2000).

Because of detraditionalization, the impact of the Christian tradition on meaning and social life has faded away and, together with the growing consciousness of religious plurality and migration, this has led to a complex and ambiguous situation of religious diversity ... Religion then can turn either into a vague religiosity – a kind of 'some-thing-ism': 'there is something more' – or a vivid and profuse 'off-piste' religious imagination, which gives rise to new religious movements borrowing from Eastern religions, the renaissance of ancient Celtic religion, different kinds of syncretisms, etc.[5]

Certainly, it needs to be acknowledged that our contemporary situation also offers Christians new possibilities to tell about their God. On a long train journey some years ago I found myself sitting opposite an avid reader. When we struck up a conversation it transpired he had a passion for philosophy. Heidegger and Camus were recently discovered intrigues. At a certain point he turned to me and, while explaining his own inability to really believe in God and the church, he said, 'Who is God for you? Tell me about your God.' It was a chance to share my experience of faith, what it means for me and how I try to live it out. He remained in contact afterwards.

Nevertheless, in the weakening of the impact of the Christian tradition in Europe, the situation is such that, as the French sociologist, Yves Lambert, has commented: 'In Europe, God is neither as dead nor as alive as some now maintain.'[6] And this points perhaps not so much to a post-modern post-secularism as rather the final outburst of modernity.

Today's 'sacred', whatever its guise, is a sacred that swallows up all absolutes. It is, as Giuseppe Zanghì puts it, a new form of nihilism that

5   See Lieven Boeve's paper at the Research Network convened by G. Ward and M. Hoelzl at the University of Manchester entitled: 'The new visibility of religion in European democratic culture' (18–20 March 2004) reproduced as 'Religion after detraditionaliza-tion: Christian faith in a post-secular Europe', *ITQ* 70 (2005), 99–122, here at p. 108.
6   Y. Lambert, 'A turning point in religious evolution in Europe', *Journal of Contemporary Religion* 19:1 (2004), 44.

moves from being rooted in the absolute that is denied to a denial that itself has become absolute. All truth claims are negated. It is no longer humanity that denies the absolute in order to affirm itself but ultimately the abso-lutising of denial that cannot but end up denying humanity itself.[7]

But why Europe? Of all the continents, why has this occurred prima-rily in Europe only then to be exported elsewhere? Why Europe, the continent that shaped such a profound and original, spiritual and artistic, philosophical, scientific and political humanism in the light of the Christian Gospel? This is our question.

A CRISIS WITHIN CHRISTIANITY

I do not pretend to provide a simple answer but I would like to offer a possible reading of what is going on. While not denying 'the mystery of iniquity' (2 Thess 2:7) that is always at work, we can also consider Europe's 'crisis' of faith as a spiritual moment of maturity within the journey of Christianity itself. This is the diagnosis of the current situation suggested by Pope John Paul II in speaking to the fifth symposium of the Bishops of Europe on 5 October 1982 when he observed:

> these tests, these temptations and this outcome of the European drama not only question Christianity and the church from outside as a diffi-culty or an external obstacle to be overcome in the work of evangelization ... but in a true sense they are interior to Christianity and the church ...

Furthermore, he notes that 'the crises of the Christian man are the crises of European man. The crises of European culture are the crises of Christian culture.' He goes right to the root of things when he concludes that 'in this light, Christianity may discover in the adventure of the European spirit

---

7   G.M. Zanghí, 'Una chiave di lettura dell'ateismo dell'Europa', *Nuova Umanità* 27:5 (2005), 625–52.

temptations, infidelities and the risks which are proper to man in his essen-tial relationship with God in Christ'.[8]

Speaking at a celebration in honour of Saint John of the Cross, Pope John Paul threw further light on what he meant by pointing to the mystical experience of, for example, someone like Saint John of the Cross. He compares the cultural crisis we are going through in Europe with a dark night which is experienced in the spiritual life. One starts with enthusiasm and great light but then undergoes a period of darkness where one's faith is deepening and maturing. The crisis of faith today is like a dark night which has acquired an epochal dimension of collective proportions.[9]

And the church is clearly caught up in this. Cardinal Connell commented in the year 2000 jubilee pastoral letter, *The knowledge of Christ,* that the misperceptions of the church is also part of this crisis of faith: 'And when the church itself is viewed as a purely human institution, a kind of bureaucracy or machine without compassion, it too is seen as a sign of the absence of God' (p. 25).

What I am proposing on the basis of Pope John Paul II's comments is that Europe's contemporary cry has something to do with the journey of Christian culture itself. This socio-spiritual and cultural 'cry' conceals a call and a hope that something new is maturing painfully in the midst of the crisis.

REDISCOVERING THE TRIUNE GOD AS OUR 'LIVING SPACE'

Can we point to what it is that might be maturing in our understanding and living out of Christianity today? In a very brief tractate, *De raptu* in *Quaestiones de veritate*, Thomas Aquinas, in commenting on how in partic-ular experiences of new communion with God, seems to indicate that God provides words in which a person can say what it is he or she is living and

---

8 'The crisis of European culture' in *Osservatore Romano* [English edition], 13 December 1982, pp 6–7.

9 Homily given during a celebration of the word in honour of Saint John of the Cross at Segovia, *Osservatore Romano* [Italian edition], 4 November 1982.

understanding – either by revealing to that person depths not yet reached in the words already used or by suggesting new words to him or her.[10] In the light of this, could it be the case that God is today leading Christians in Europe to understand words we already use but have not fully grasped? Or, indeed, is opening up new insights into divine revelation as explained by Vatican II's document on Revelation, *Dei Verbum*, 8?

Here I would like to refer briefly to one specific example – the central doctrine of our faith: the triune God, the Trinity.[11] It's as if today God is responding by bringing us to rediscover him as a divine community of love. To speak of the person of Christ is to speak of the Trinity. We have great dogmas concerning Christ and Trinity. But how far have we let ourselves, our thinking, our acting be informed and penetrated by these mysteries? How far have these truths of faith managed to become what they deep down are: also anthropological truths, truths that are historical and social, to be 'done' in charity?

Perhaps the current crisis is opening up for us a deeper, living articulation of these truths. We know that at the origins of modernity, Immanuel Kant considered the Christian doctrine of the Trinity as a piece of useless speculation.[12] The Italian theologian, now archbishop, Bruno Forte writes of centuries which suffered an 'exile of the Trinity'.[13] Karl Rahner, Hans Urs von Balthasar and others point to the shocking observation that what we claim to be the central doctrine of our faith, the Trinity impinges hardly at all on our understanding and our everyday living of the faith: 'We must be willing to admit that, should the doctrine of the Trinity have to be dropped as false, the major part of religious literature could well remain virtually unchanged.'[14]

And yet, the trinitarian horizon is central to our faith! In Jesus Christ

---

10   Thomas Aquinas, 'Rapture' in *Truth II: Questions X-XX*, trans. J.V. McGlynn (Indianapolis/Cambridge, 1954), pp 180–206.

11   *Catechism of the Catholic church*, n. 234.

12   I. Kant, *The conflict of the faculties*, trans. Mary Gregor (Lincoln, NB, 1992).

13   *Trinity as history: saga of the Christian God* (New York, 1989), pp 3–4.

14   K. Rahner, *The Trinity* (London, 1970), pp 10–15. See also H.U. von Balthasar, *The glory of the Lord*, V (Edinburgh, 1991), p. 23; J. O'Donnell, 'Revelation and Trinity,' in *The mystery of the triune God* (London, 1988), pp 17–39.

we discover a whole anthropology of communion, a trinitarian anthropology, a way of living that is modelled on the trinitarian relationships that
God lives in himself. The triune God is nothing less than our true 'living
space'.

LIVING THE TRINITY

A priest I know told me of how some years ago at a moment of crisis in his
life he met a group of young people who were trying to really live out their
faith. He was struck by their life. To his question: 'What do you do?' one of
them answered, 'We live the Trinity.' This response amazed him and began
his journey out of the crisis.

It's as if today, Europe, like Job, is struggling as a continent not simply
with an abstract notion of God but with the revelation of the triune God in
Jesus Christ. Or is it also the case that God today 'struggles' with Europeans
to make his life of communion, dialogue and trinitarian *perichòresis* be
welcomed more deeply by them in order to welcome them more deeply
into himself, so that we might 'live the Trinity' at all levels?

What are the signs that there is a new discovery of this true triune face
of God? Well, firstly, it is not by coincidence that there has been a huge
blossoming of theological and spiritual writings concerning the Trinity in
all traditions. Some names of theological and spiritual writers on this
theme spring to mind: Sergius Bulgakov, Yves Congar, Anne Fatula, Colin
Gunter, Eberhard Jüngel, Anne Hunt, Chiara Lubich, Jürgen Moltmann,
Karl Rahner, Hans Urs von Balthasar, Adrienne von Speyr, Simon Weil and
John Zizioulous. Most authoritatively we read in the apostolic exhortation
Ecclesia in Europa written after the 1999 synod to which Cardinal Connell
contributed:

> [the church] has the task of reviving faith in the Trinity among the
> Christians of Europe, knowing full well that this faith is the herald of
> authentic hope for the continent. Many of the great paradigms of refer-
> ence ..., which are at the core of European civilization, have their

deepest roots in the Church's trinitarian faith. This faith contains an extraordinary spiritual, cultural and ethical potential which is also capable of shedding light on some of the more important questions discussed in Europe today, such as social disintegration and the loss of a meaningful point of reference for life and history. Hence the need for a renewed theological, spiritual and pastoral meditation on the mystery of the Trinity (no. 19).

The Second Vatican Council clearly underlined the trinitarian mystery of the church. The words and deeds of our recent popes of the Council – Paul VI, John Paul II and, now, Benedict XVI – have echoed this in many different ways. They do so by underlining how contemplation of the Trinity has direct implications for the church and our living of the gospel in society.

Most recently, in his encyclical letter, *Deus caritas est*, Pope Benedict has underscored charity in every aspect of the church's life (Interestingly, Cardinal Connell's first pastoral letter as archbishop was *Witnessing to God's love*.) The pope quotes Augustine in a wonderful summary: *si vides caritatem, vides trinitatem* (if you see love, you see the Trinity):

> 'If you see charity, you see the Trinity' . . . The entire activity of the church is an expression of a love that seeks the integral good of man. . . Love of neighbour, grounded in the love of God, is first and foremost a responsibility for each individual member of the faithful, but it is also a responsibility for the entire ecclesial community at every level: from the local community to the particular Church and to the Church universal in its entirety. As a community, the Church must practise love (nos. 19–20).

In this setting, we might also recall Pope John Paul's blueprint for the third millennium, *Novo millennio ineunte*, 43: 'To make the church the home and the school of communion [and here Pope John Paul was referring to what he called "living the Trinity," cf. *NMI*, 29]: that is the great challenge facing us in the millennium which is now beginning.'

To create lively pockets of true, living communion requires, however, promoting a spirituality of communion. And what is this spirituality of communion? Pope John Paul provides its contours. It is our 'heart's contemplation of the mystery of the Trinity dwelling in us, and whose light we must also be able to see shining on the face of the brothers and sisters around us'. It means 'an ability to think of our brothers and sisters in faith within the profound unity of the Mystical Body, and therefore as "those who are a part of me"'. It makes us 'able to share their joys and sufferings, to sense their desires and attend to their needs, to offer them deep and genuine friendship'. A spirituality of communion implies also the ability to see what is positive in others, to welcome it and prize it as a gift from God: not only as a gift for the brother or sister who has received it directly, but also as a gift for me. A spirituality of communion means . . . to know how to make room for our brothers and sisters, bearing 'each other's burdens'.

Centuries ago, Pachomius, a Roman solider, returning after a battle, was struck by people he saw coming out of their houses and taking care of the wounded. He asked who they were and in discovering they were Christians, he converted. It's up to us now to manifest moments of mutual love, genuine spheres of communion that are transparent to the triune God of mutual love in whom we believe.

LABORATORIES OF COMMUNION

Vatican II, the teaching of the popes, the social doctrine of the church as well as theological and spiritual writers are all pointing us in the direction of rediscovering and living the Trinity. But it is also true that the triune God has not only responded by underlining this doctrinally. He has also responded in another way too. Through the Holy Spirit, new charisms have emerged that have given rise to new communities, movements and groups. These are also helping the church to underline how Christianity is a communitarian reality. They are like creative laboratories of this programme.[15]

15   Pontifical Council for the Laity, *Movements in the Church* (Vatican, 1999).

The Holy Spirit has aroused in men and women of our time new and relevant experiences of the gospel of Jesus that open up windows for us onto the gospel. The history of the church is full of similar examples as the then Cardinal Joseph Ratzinger highlighted in 1998 at a congress of these new communities and which now as pope he is underlining again as he calls these movements together at Pentecost this year (2006).[16] There have been interesting developments too between Catholic movements and communities and movements of other churches as seen in the large European gathering of Stuttgart in 2004 and again this will be repeated in 2007.[17]

In the past, when there arose outcries on this continent of Europe, new communities came to life around figures such as Benedict, Francis, Dominic, Catherine of Siena, Teresa of Avila and Ignatius of Loyola. They provided extraordinary impulses in their times. Perhaps God has not forgotten our times, but it is important we be attentive to what 'the Spirit is saying to the church' (Rev 2:7).

THE MYSTERIOUS CRY THAT ANSWERS OUR CRY

So far we have proposed a reading of what might be maturing within European's Christian culture. But Europe's cry is answered most poignantly, perhaps, in another cry – that of Jesus on the cross who himself cried out 'Why?' This cry is what John Paul II called the 'mystery within the mystery' of Christ.[18] It is the cry that paradoxically reveals the most the very life of mutual love between the persons of the Trinity because it is

16   J. Ratzinger, 'The theological locus of ecclesial movements,' *Communio* (Fall, 1998), 480–504.

17   The 'Together for Europe' meeting took place in Stuttgart, Germany on 8 May 2004 with approximately 9,000 participants, among them 50 bishops from various churches and many politicians. Around 100,000 people followed the meeting thanks to satellite link-ups with meetings taking place contemporaneously in 135 European cities. The proceedings of the Meeting were published in English, Italian and German by Città Nuova, Rome.

18   *Novo millennio ineunte*, 25.

when Jesus is loving the most in fidelity to his mission towards the Father and towards us.

It is again significant that in our time artists, literary writers, psychologists, theologians and spiritual writers have drawn our attention to that moment of the cross where Jesus cries out his sense of being abandoned by the Father. The work of the artist, Francis Bacon, comes to mind. It is the cry that opens up for us our entrance into the triune life of God as Cardinal Connell wrote in *The knowledge of Christ* (p. 22): 'Jesus' cry on the cross: "My God, my God, why hast thou forsaken me?" (Mt 27:46) . . . At that moment he felt as if displaced and evicted from the depths of his being: he knew what it was to feel cut off from home. And to what purpose? That he might return home with us.'

Heidegger once wrote that a turning point will only come if we recognise the abyss. But for this to happen there have to be people to reach the abyss. Jesus on the cross cries out in abandonment. He is the man who has touched the deepest and most desolate roots of our human creaturehood, right to the point of abandonment by God. He felt distance, confusion, lack of belonging. His too was a cry of uncertainty, weariness and darkness. But Jesus crucified and forsaken is God who has reached humanity in the depths of being deprived of light in order to open us and bring us to the light.

So, in Jesus crucified and forsaken, we can re-read our current situation. Yes, the 'negative' of Europe's contemporary cry is certainly negative – I cannot deny darkness is darkness – but it is also the 'promise' of a novelty of life – of a resurrection – as big as is the crisis.

Each of us, however, feels the wounds of our time and culture. We all participate in that existential angst. Each of us has a sense of being at times on the knife-edge of the cultural crisis that touches deeply in our own personal lives. And that is why each of us is called to recognise, name and love Jesus crucified and forsaken because, in so doing each of us, and all together, can contribute to the emergence of a culture of the resurrection for today.

It requires we be people who hear the contemporary cry of our culture with one ear but with the other ear hear the cry of the crucified and forsaken Christ. As one spiritual writer of our times, Chiara Lubich, puts it, Jesus crucified and forsaken is:

> speech for the mute, the answer for the unknowing, light for the blind, a voice for the deaf, rest for the weary, hope for the despairing, satisfaction for the hungry, reality for the deceived ... victory for the failure, certainty for the uncertain, normality for the strange, company for the lonely ... He assumed forsakenness by God; therefore God is close even when we think we have been forsaken by him.[19]

CONCLUSION

I started off by noting Europe's cry of theoretical and practical atheism. In his 1993 pastoral letter, Christ our life (p. 113) Cardinal Connell noted how the 1991 synod on Europe recognised this. He quoted the synodal declaration: '[Jesus'] entire life, culminating in the Easter mystery of his death and resurrection, proclaims the truth: God loves you, Jesus Christ came for your sake' (no. 3).

I have proposed that this proclamation involves the rediscovery of the trinitarian face of God who is love, mutual love and so also our living out a spirituality of communion. All of this is made possible for us, however, if we nourish ourselves on the Eucharist, the great gift from heaven that Cardinal Connell never ceased to proclaim. In the Eucharist we meet Jesus Crucified and Forsaken who brings us into the new life of mutual love in the heart of the Father.

In his jubilee pastoral letter, The knowledge of Christ, Cardinal Connell provided us with a wonderful meditation on the link between friendship, love, knowledge of Christ and the eucharist. In 'the "today" of Christ's life in the church' the Cardinal wrote, we are invited into 'our imperishable dwelling with the Father "in the unity of the Holy Spirit" at the heart of the church' (pp. 19–21).

---

19   C. Lubich, The Cry (London, 2001), pp 48–50.

Oliver Clément, the contemporary Orthodox writer has written: 'I am really convinced that Christianity is still young; the world hasn't seen anything yet.'[20] The church has always been rejuvenated by the Holy Spirit. And the 'today' of the church is no exception. The words of the prophet Isaiah provide a conclusion of hope: 'No need to recall the past, no need to think about what was done before. See, I am doing a new deed, even now it comes to light'(Is 45:18–19).

20   See R. Migliorini interview with Oliver Clément in *Avvenire*, 1 October 2003.

Imagination and affectivity: response to the postmodern cry

MICHAEL PAUL GALLAGHER SJ

I BEGIN BY EXPRESSING MY GRATITUDE and happiness to have this opportunity to pay tribute to Cardinal Connell. Our lives overlapped in University College Dublin for some twenty years, because we were both among the handful of priests on the faculty of that large state university. I was in the English department and Professor Connell of course was in philosophy. From my memories of those years I want to offer one simple testimony. Father Connell, as he was usually known, was universally appreciated among his colleagues. Not everyone in such a secular institution agreed with him on every issue, but everyone knew him to be a gentleman and a gentle man. So it is with those happy recollections in the background that I offer my short response to the paper we have just heard.

Needless to say I agree with what Father Leahy has so well elaborated and I want only to suggest two additional horizons that could be relevant. He has invited us to recognize in our Christian image of God as Trinity a powerful answer to the anthropological crisis of Europe, in other words as offering a healing of our damaged self-images. Instead of a sense of ourselves as *imago Dei*, today's Europe, I would say, has suffered three major wounds. Many people now find themselves in a lonely cultural desolation without roots of belonging. Besides, their lifestyle often leaves them kidnapped by pragmatic immediacies and unable to hear their hearts and spirits. And thirdly, their self-images can become shrunken into private spaces and thus closed to the cry of pain around them. Is it possible to link the healing of these wounds with God as Trinity? Over thirty years ago, the then Professor Joseph Ratzinger wrote that 'God is not loneliness but ecstasy.' Indeed, the same term 'ecstasy' recurs in paragraph 6 of his recent encyclical. And he added: 'The mystery of the Trinity has opened a completely new perspective, showing us that the ground of being is communion.' In this light our Christian hope is to invite people to ponder and pray the differentness of God as Trinity. But how? How can we incarnate or inculturate this treasured revelation of God?

To initiate an answer to that difficult pastoral question, I propose two key words, each of them borrowed from a cardinal. From Cardinal Newman, who of course was the 'only begetter' of the university where Cardinal Connell and myself both taught for many years, I take the term 'imagination'. From Cardinal Scola, present patriarch of Venice, I take the term 'affectivity', and I want to suggest, with extreme brevity, that these two areas could be of special religious importance for the culture of our postmodern Europe.

Newman, especially in his *Grammar of assent*, broke new ground with his positive interpretation of the role of imagination on the road to faith. Perhaps his most famous statement was that 'the heart is commonly reached, not through the reason, but through the imagination', and he went on to claim that our faith needs to be 'appropriated as a reality by the religious imagination'. Again, if people's 'imaginations are not at all kindled', then 'the truths' about God will not come alive, will remain notional, will not 'live in their imagination'. In short, and this is still a powerful insight 136 years later, lives are not really transformed until God's truth touches people's imagination. In postmodern culture, a theme that could be developed at length, the crisis of faith is more on this level of sensibility than of ideas, and at the same time one promising aspect of postmodern culture is to revalue the role of sensibility and of imagination in our making or discovery of meaning.

A few months ago Cardinal Angelo Scola spoke of an 'anthropological transformation in which we are immersed' and which invites us to revisit and rethink our fundamental experience of affectivity. He added that the relationship between affectivity and faith today is as important for us as the relationship between revolution and faith in the nineteenth century. Although everyone can recognise a pseudo-romantic danger in some of the contemporary cult of affectivity, nevertheless it is a field that, together with spirituality, is being increasingly explored by theologians of today, notably by Pierangelo Sequeri here in Italy. Affectivity and imagination are twin aspects of our human adventure of meaning that are being retrieved and re-appreciated in this postmodern moment (partly because, like religious faith itself, they were despised or neglected by a narrow form of modernity).

Although these two words do not appear in *Deus caritas est*, it is not untrue to say that this first encyclical of Pope Benedict XVI aims at reimag-ining the full range of our love, or affectivity, and in this way healing the wounds of our self-images. In this session we have been asking how the high doctrine of the Trinity might possibly heal our anthropological ills. Our honoured guest of this evening, Cardinal Connell, gave a lecture some three years ago at Strawberry Hill, London, in which he touched on that question. He discerned three cries of our culture and suggested a set of parallels with the blessed Trinity. All thirst for life, ultimately for eternal life, finds its fulfillment in the Father. The need to belong is met by the companionship of Our Lord Jesus Christ. The quest for meaning is guided, within us, by the gift of the Holy Spirit.

Where can that rich vision find language for today? My suggestion has been at the crossroads between our imagination and our affectivity. More concretely still, more than many of our struggling words, perhaps ten minutes of prayerful attention before the most famous icon in the world, Rublev's Trinity, could invite people into that circle of love which ulti-mately is our triune God. Because if one enters the fourth space at that table, our imagination can be healed and our affectivity transformed by what the Holy Father calls the 'love-story' between God and all of us. And then we as *communio* and *caritas* can echo and embody that mystery which we glimpse – for the healing of hope in our wounded history.

Words of introduction

CARDINAL ANGELO SODANO

Your Eminence,
Dear friends,

I thought it my duty to join you this evening because of the deep respect and esteem I have always had for our dear Cardinal Desmond Connell and for his successor as archbishop of Dublin, Monsignor Diarmuid Martin. It is also a great pleasure for me to come again to the Pontifical Irish College, because of the various bonds which I have with it and because of all that the College represents in the long history of the Catholic church in Ireland.

In a few weeks, Cardinal Connell celebrates his eightieth birthday. On behalf of the Holy Father, Pope Benedict XVI, and the College of Cardinals, of which he is a distinguished member, I wish him a very happy birthday. As he gives thanks to almighty God for all that he has received over the years as a priest and bishop, I ask that God will continue to bless him with good health and every happiness.

The Irish College has decided to honour Cardinal Connell in a most appropriate way with this set of talks on issues of philosophy and theology. It is my pleasure to introduce the final talk of this afternoon's colloquium by Archbishop William Joseph Levada, who will soon be raised to the dignity of cardinal. He will share his learning with us on the theme 'The diocesan bishop and the universal magisterium'. I have no doubt that the next hour or so will be a special time of spiritual joy and illumination for us all.

The diocesan bishop and the universal magisterium

CARDINAL WILLIAM JOSEPH LEVADA

T HE SUBJECT ASSIGNED TO ME for this colloquium in honour of Cardinal Connell has for its title 'The diocesan bishop and the universal magisterium.' On 13 May 2005, I was appointed prefect of the Congregation for the Doctrine of the Faith, on which Cardinal Connell has served as a member for these past thirteen years. The topic no doubt seemed a natural one in view of the cardinal's service as a diocesan bishop who has regularly participated in this one aspect of the exercise of the universal magisterium, that is, in the ordinary magisterium of the pope who also exercises his teaching authority through the instructions and decrees of the congregation. If that is the genesis for my presentation, it provides me once again the happy opportunity to offer gratitude to Cardinal Connell on behalf of the members and staff of the congregation, on my own behalf as the new prefect, and on behalf of our former prefect, Pope Benedict, who asked me to offer his thanks to you personally during my audience with him last evening.

The framework for speaking about the bishop and the universal magisterium is twofold: the apostolic college, the members of which were called by Jesus Christ to be the foundation stones upon which his church is built, and were sent by him to implement the mission for which God the Father sent his Son into the world, on the one hand; and on the other the deposit of faith, 'the Gospel' they were sent to preach – the 'Gospel' in the Pauline sense that forms the content of the church's magisterium. Early on in Mark's Gospel we read that Jesus 'went up the mountain and called to him those whom he wanted, and they came to him. And he appointed twelve, whom he also named apostles, to be with him, and to be sent out to proclaim the gospel' (Mk 3: 13–14). The three synoptic gospels finish with some account of that 'sending out': 'And he said to them, "Go into the whole world and proclaim the good news to the whole creation" ... And they went out and proclaimed the good news everywhere, and the Lord worked with them' (Mk 16: 15, 20).

In view of such a topic, the student of theology will immediately think of *Lumen gentium,* the dogmatic constitution on the church of the Second Vatican Council, the fortieth anniversary of whose conclusion was marked on the solemnity of the Immaculate Conception last December. The rich legacy of the council's four sessions offers us a sure guide in many areas of church life, most certainly in its thorough presentation of a comprehensive ecclesiology for our time. In the council's reflection on the nature and mission of the church in *Lumen gentium,* the third chapter treats of the apostolic character of the church, but only after the splendid vision of the spiritual reality of the church as mystery – as communion with the divine Trinity through the mission of Christ and his Holy Spirit – and of the resulting descriptive identity of the church as one, holy and catholic has been presented.

At the beginning of *Lumen gentium* we read that 'the church, in Christ, is like a sacrament – a sign and instrument, that is, of communion with God and of the unity of the entire human race' (*LG,* 1). To call the church a 'sacrament' was novel at the time: the *Catechism of the Catholic Church* provides this succinct but profound commentary on the point:

> Christ himself is the mystery of salvation ... The saving word of his holy and sanctifying humanity is the sacrament of salvation, which is revealed and active in the church's sacraments ... The seven sacraments are the signs and instruments by which the Holy Spirit spreads the grace of Christ the head throughout the church which is his body. The church, then, both contains and communicates the invisible grace she signifies. It is in this analogical sense, that the church is called a sacrament (*CCC,* 774).

I have referred to the Council's use of the sacramental analogy in its description of the church because it provides the foundation for a discussion of the council's teaching on the hierarchical nature of the church in chapter three, especially in view of the important clarification of church teaching about the sacramental nature of episcopal ordination. The council puts an end to past controversy in regard to the office of bishop by teaching that the bishop is not just a priest with greater powers of jurisdiction, but that he receives through sacramental consecration the fullness of the power of orders, which inherently gives him the power to teach, sanctify and govern. This teaching also points to the way in which the insights of biblical and patristic studies helped the council fathers overcome an overly juridical approach to the nature of the church and its hierarchy: the concept of 'sacrament' – a visible reality that communicates invisible grace – helps to hold in focus both the spiritual and institutional features of the church – the Body of the incarnate Word.

Perhaps it will be helpful at this point to recall the overview *Lumen gentium* provides about what it intends to set forth in chapter 3:

> This holy synod, following the steps of the first Vatican Council, with it teaches and declares that Jesus Christ, the eternal pastor established the holy church by sending the apostles as he himself had been sent by the Father (see John 20:21). He willed that their successors, the bishops, should be the shepherds in his church until the end of the world. In order that the episcopate itself, however, might be one and undivided he placed blessed Peter over the other apostles, and in him he set up a lasting and visible source and foundation of the unity both of faith and of communion. This teaching on the institution, the permanence, the nature and the force of the sacred primacy of the Roman Pontiff and his infallible teaching office, the sacred synod proposes anew to be firmly believed by all the faithful. Further, continuing with this same undertaking, it intends to profess before all and to declare the teaching on bishops, successors of the apostles, who together with Peter's successor, the Vicar of Christ and the visible head of the whole church, govern the house of the living God (*LG*, 18).

It is this teaching on bishops, of course, that is the new development offered by the Second Vatican Council in respect to the first.

Karl Rahner calls article 22 of *Lumen gentium* on the college of bishops 'one of the central themes of the whole council'.[1] It is not a teaching that departs from theological tradition; what is new is that here for the first time it is taught explicitly by the highest authority of the church, i.e. the apostolic college of bishops itself. In summary, the council teaches:

1) There exists an order or 'college' of bishops. About this fact, Rahner says that the word should be understood to mean 'that the episcopate as a whole and its powers are not just the sum of individual bishops and their powers. As a juridical personality, sacramentally based and hence sustained by the Spirit of God, this inclusive unity precedes (objectively) the individual bishops as such.' Further, the 'power of the individual bishop as an individual – the threefold office – is to be regarded as coming to him insofar as he is a member of the college and sharer in the power of the college as such.'[2]

2) This college continues the college of apostles. Although *Lumen gentium* does not say of the college of bishops what it says of the college of apostles, i.e. that it is founded by the divine will, the indication that the apostolic college will continue to the end of the world is sufficient to say that the apostolic succession of the college of bishops is also considered to be *iure divino*.

3) The college exists only insofar as it has the pope as its head, and hence as an 'intrinsic element' constitutive of its being. One cannot properly speak of the college with the pope as its head, and the college 'alone' without the pope; on the other hand, one *can* distinguish between the college with the pope as its head and the pope acting alone. Even in this latter case, as we can see from the practice of inquiring among the bishops before the papal definitions of Pius IX and XII, and before Pope John Paul II's solemn teaching about abortion and euthanasia in *Evangelium vitae*, it is possible to say of such solemn papal teaching that the pope is teaching as head of the college of bishops.

1   K. Rahner, 'Commentary on the Constitution on the Church,' in H. Vorgrimler (ed.), *Commentary on the documents of Vatican II*, I (New York, 1967), p. 195.

2   Ibid., p. 198.

4) The college of bishops (with the pope as its head) possesses supreme and full authority over the whole church. The ecumenical council is the instance cited in this section of the Council's teaching: these councils were the decisive consideration in acknowledging the existence of the college of bishops.

5) The exercise of the authority of the college must be a 'collegiate' act, hence always in some way involving the cooperation of its head, the pope.

Since by ordination a bishop becomes a member of the apostolic college, and shares in the supreme authority over the universal church – always in union with the head of the college, the pope – it follows that this responsibility is preeminently found in his exercise of the universal magisterium or teaching authority. The ecumenical councils are the primary historical manifestations of this responsibility. But the ecumenical council does not exhaust this responsibility, which can also find expression in synodal actions and collaborative efforts to teach and safeguard the deposit of faith on the part of the college of bishops. The teaching of the First Vatican Council on the 'ordinary and universal magisterium' points to yet another instance of the exercise of this responsibility. Moreover, the bishop as pastor of a particular church not only symbolically but also practically is the apostolic link to the church universal, not only 'synchronically' (with the apostolic college of today) but 'diachronically' (with the apostolic college back to the apostles themselves). So we shall return to article 25 of *Lumen gentium* for a further look at the issue of the bishop's teaching authority or magisterium.

The key teaching of the council about the magisterium or teaching authority of the bishop in and for the church is found in *Lumen gentium*, 25, which preaching of the gospel 'occupies an eminent place'. It goes on to call the bishops 'authentic teachers, that is, teachers endowed with the authority of Christ'. This preeminent teaching role is often referred to as the 'ordinary magisterium' of the diocesan bishop as pastor of a particular church. His teaching is the guarantee of the 'tradition' or handing on of the deposit of faith in his local church; as a result, it is a witness to the 'universal magisterium' of the church. Indeed, the council teaches (*Dei Verbum*, 10) that 'the task of authentically interpreting the word of God, whether written or handed on, has been entrusted exclusively to the living teaching office of the church'; hence to the diocesan bishop, whose teaching does not participate in the charism of infallibility in its exercise. But since 'the faith' is by its nature one – Ephesians underscores the Church's unity: 'There is one Lord, one faith, one baptism' (4:5) – the bishop's ordinary magisterium will involve teaching what has been infallibly proposed, taught, and received as the deposit of faith, the very gospel of our Lord.

The council introduces the classic teaching on the universal ordinary magisterium as an instance of this 'infallible' teaching:

> Although the individual bishops do not enjoy the prerogative of infalli-bility, they can nevertheless proclaim Christ's doctrine infallibly. This is so, even when they are dispersed around the world, provided that while maintaining the bond *of* unity among themselves and with Peter's successor, and while teaching authentically on a matter *of* faith or morals, they concur in a single viewpoint as the one which must be held conclusively [*definitive tenendam*] (*LG*, 25).

This is common doctrine, but still lacks clarity on the modality of recog-nising when one may be able to say about a particular doctrine that it is infallibly guaranteed by the universal ordinary magisterium. I cited above as an example of universal ordinary magisterium John Paul's encyclical *Evangelium vitae*, 62 in which he says,

> By the authority which Christ conferred upon Peter and his Successors, in communion with the bishops – who on various occasions have condemned abortion and who in the aforementioned consultation, albeit dispersed throughout the world, have shown unanimous agree-ment concerning this doctrine – I declare that direct abortion, that is, abortion willed as an end or as a means, always constitutes a grave moral disorder, since it is the deliberate killing *of* an innocent human being. This doctrine is based upon the natural law and upon the written Word of God, is transmitted by the church's tradition and taught by the ordinary and universal magisterium.'

It is clear that the pope intended here to declare that the church teaching about the evil of abortion is part of infallible church teaching, *definitive tenendam* by reason of universal ordinary magisterium. Moreover, a classic example of the ordinary and universal magisterium is the Apostles Creed.

Father Frank Sullivan, a professor in my time at the Gregorian University, posited an interesting theory about some of the teachings of Vatican II itself, specifically the teachings of chapter three of *Lumen gentium* on the sacramental nature of episcopal ordination, and the college of bishops. Although the council described itself as 'pastoral' in nature, and thus did not employ the form of infallible dogmatic declarations, it did distinguish clear doctrinal positions on these two issues by the phrase 'This sacred synod teaches that . . .' Sullivan hypothesised that since this was clear teaching by the world's bishops – not dispersed but gathered in council – it would be difficult not to recognise it as fulfilling the criteria for infallible teaching by the ordinary and universal magisterium. Perhaps in the future other instances of the bishops' collegial action, such as the synod of bishops, will have a role in helping to identify such teaching by the ordinary and universal magisterium.

The final category for our consideration today is that of papal teaching. I take it for granted that infallible papal definitions (sometimes referred to as extraordinary papal magisterium) are clearly seen as an exercise of the 'universal magisterium'. With regard to the far more common exercise of papal teaching, the ordinary papal magisterium, this too should be regarded as 'universal', at least when the manner and subject matter of the teaching do not show it to have a particular destination. To such teaching, according to the Council, all the faithful must give 'religious submission of will and of mind', a reverence that respects the guidance of the Holy Spirit promised to blessed Peter and his successors in an habitual way, even when they are not making an infallible declaration. We should recall that more solemn ordinary papal teaching usually deals with matters that are part of the deposit of faith, or have a necessary connection with it or its defence and proper understanding.

In regard to such papal teaching, the bishop has a unique role as spokesman. His links with the Holy Father as a member of the one apostolic college give him a principal share in the effective diffusion of such papal magisterial statements. The reception of papal teaching is never something automatic, and the faithful rely on their pastor to guide them into a deeper understanding of it, especially in its application to their own situation.

By way of conclusion to these reflections, I want to recall the address our Holy Father Pope Benedict XVI gave to the Roman Curia just before Christmas. Noting how difficult the implementation of the Second Vatican Council has been is some parts of the Church, the pope said that such problems regarding its proper implementation arose 'from the fact that two contrary hermeneutics [or interpretations of the council] came face to face and quarreled with each other'. He called these two interpretations a 'hermeneutic of discontinuity and rupture' on the one hand, in which the post-conciliar church stands opposed to the pre-conciliar church, and a 'hermeneutic of reform' which seeks renewal but always in continuity with the tradition of the church.

I hope my reflections this afternoon have in some small way been able to show how the Second Vatican Council itself, reflecting its true 'spirit'. sought just such a hermeneutic of reform in continuity in addressing some of the pressing issues before it. Furthermore, it is precisely in the ongoing papal teaching that we can find the most faithful such 'hermeneutic of reform' by which the Council can rightly be interpreted; I think here of the rich treasury of papal encyclicals, of post-synodal apostolic exhortations, of instructions – not excluding the many documents of the Congregation for the Doctrine of the Faith through which the popes have exercised their magisterium over these past forty years.

Finally, I want to call attention to a phrase from the first Vatican Council's Decree *Pastor aeternus* that caught my attention during my preparation of these remarks. The introductory words of that decree about papal primacy and infallibility are taken from 1 Peter 2:25: 'You had gone astray like sheep, but you have now returned to the shepherd and guardian of your souls.' The word 'guardian' translates the word *episkopon* in the original Greek. So the Latin text of the decree begins *'Pastor aeternus et epis-*

copus animarum nostrarum'. It seems a beautiful thing when talking about bishops and popes to be reminded that all the faithful, from pope to youngest infant, have a 'bishop' who looks after us. It is Jesus Christ, the eternal shepherd and bishop of our souls!

The sacramental nature
of the episcopal office

CARDINAL DESMOND CONNELL

Your Eminence,
Your Excellency, Archbishop Levada,
Your Excellencies and my dear brothers and sisters.

IT IS APPROPRIATE FOR ME, I think, before I make any comment on what we have just heard to express my gratitude for all that has been done to honour me as I approach my eightieth birthday. It was the goodness of the Irish College that conceived this idea and I want to express my deep gratitude to the rector and to the vice-rector and the staff of the Irish College. They have presented me with something that I had never imagined, which I have found somewhat embarrassing, but which has given me immense joy and immense happiness. and I thank the Irish College from my heart.

I have loved the Irish College. I wasn't a Roman. I was in Louvain. I wasn't in Rome at all as a student. I visited Rome as a tourist on three or four occasions. I was at Archbishop Ryan's consecration by Pope Paul VI. That was as much as I knew of Rome. But the Irish College took me into its heart when I became archbishop of Dublin. And I will always remember the way in which Archbishop Brady, who was rector at the time, and subsequently Bishop John Fleming, and the vice-rectors; how they helped me and how they made me so warmly welcome so that I did feel I was so at home here. And how easily I moved among students here in the College. It has been a lovely experience for me and I want to express my deepest gratitude to the Irish College.

But on this particular occasion this evening, I want to express my appreciation to His Eminence Cardinal Sodano. When I saw that the secretary of state would be guiding one of the meetings, I was over-whelmed. And I do thank Your Eminence from my heart for your graciousness in coming to this meeting which is part of what was intended to be in honour of me. I will always remember how deeply indebted I am to Your Eminence.

Archbishop Levada has just given our talk. Yes, we have been colleagues at the Congregation for the Doctrine of the Faith and over the years we have known one another, but tonight I want, first of all, to express my congratulations to him on his appointment as the prefect at the Congregation for the Doctrine of the Faith and also now his appointment as cardinal. I want to say how greatly I rejoice in his promotion in these very significant ways. Archbishop Levada, soon to be Cardinal Levada, will be one of the most important people in Rome, one of the most important people in the Curia. He has been given a great responsibility and I am quite certain, knowing him as I do, that he will fulfil those responsibilities with great – I won't just simply say – success but with something more than success, which comes from the grace of God. I know that will very much be the future under Cardinal Levada, as he is to be.

I want to express my deepest gratitude to my own archbishop. How good of him it is to come here. I know how busy he is, and I know how many things he has to do. One of the lovely things that I have experienced since I retired from office has been that communion between us, and I want to say that the archbishop has been to me so kind and so good, so thoughtful in so many different ways, and I want publicly to declare how I deeply appreciate that and how grateful I am in my heart. It is marvellous that we should be together as brothers in the diocese, each of us in his own proper sphere.

I also want to thank everybody else who has come here, the speakers, including my own former colleague in UCD who is still very much a meta-physician. I do appreciate your coming and what you have given us in your paper and the professor who responded. I also want to thank Fr Breandán. I'm not sure – I think you were already ordained when I became arch-bishop [*BL: just that year*]. Yes, I think so. But I could see that I had somebody very special when I met you. And then I met you here in Rome when you were doing your doctorate and from that time on. But thank you for the paper you have given and your kind remarks and also Bishop Brian Farrell. I am deeply grateful to you all.

Now, Archbishop Levada has given us an outline of the teaching of the church on the diocesan bishop and the universal magisterium. What he has given us is both lucid and comprehensive and I find it not easy to know what it would be appropriate for me to say here. I am so happy to hear him speak of the sacramental nature of the episcopal office. I think that is tremendously important. The episcopal office is not simply a matter of jurisdiction, not simply a matter of the organisation of the church. It is not just simply a matter of who has power as so often seems to be assumed. The episcopal office is something of tremendous importance within the church for its sacramental nature. And the sacramental nature includes the teaching responsibility of the bishop. So we are thinking of something that is of very great significance which requires of the bishop not just that he should know his theology – and that is required of all bishops – but that he should be a man of prayer, that he should be a man whose teaching comes from communion with the Lord. And that seems to me to be of very great importance in the question of the universal ordinary magisterium.

Now the second thing that strikes me as very important from what the prefect has said concerns the college of bishops. The college of bishops is something of very great importance that came to prominence at the Second Vatican Council. The Holy Father when he addressed us on the morning following his election spoke very warmly about collegiality and his communion with the bishops, and he invited the bishops to help him. And that collegiality is something of very great importance and significance in the life of the church because it is an expression of communion.

How it is to be expressed and implemented is the difficulty because the church is now such a vast body spread throughout the world. That is one side of it. The other side of it is that everything has become so much smaller by reason of communications. You cannot imagine the Holy See being in touch with every bishop in the second or third century. Now the Holy See is immediately present to every diocese in the world through communications. So at the same time you have the vastness and the compactness. And how collegiality is to be expressed in these circumstances it is very difficult to know. For example, one does sometimes hear that what we want is – oh – what's this they call it? When you reach my age . . . [*laughter*] getting away from a very tight unity to a more . . . decentralisation. And yet decentralisation has to be considered in the light that what Bishop *A* might have to say in the most remote places, if it happens to be something which he shouldn't say, it is on television screens throughout the world. So what does decentralisation mean, how can decentralisation be realised? I am in favour of decentralisation in the sense of calling on each and every one to exercise his responsibilities, personal responsibilities for each bishop to live his personal responsibility. Certainly, and that is how I understand decentralisation. But the decentralisation that leads to independent freedoms is an entirely different matter.

The Holy Father has certainly spoken to the cardinals in a way which indicates, and of course in a way his critics would never have anticipated, and it does indicate a desire on the part of the Holy Father to find the right way to express collegiality within the church. I do believe that that is going to be very important for the future. There is another matter that the prefect raised concerning the universal ordinary magisterium as an instance of infallible teaching and the prefect referred to *Evangelium vitae*. One thing that I have found difficult throughout my episcopate was a certain kind of theologian who seems to look on magisterial statements as if they were first of all to be put under the microscope to see if they are infallible, if they fulfil all the requirements for an infallible statement. If they don't, and of course normally they don't seem to, then the teaching is 'offered for our consideration' and not for our acceptance, and that for me has been unacceptable. The teaching of the magisterium, it seems to me, requires our acceptance and it is not just for our consideration.

If you take another case – the prefect raised *Evangelium vitae* and the issue of abortion – but I can think of another case: *Ordinatio sacerdotalis*, where the pope spoke in the most direct way – at least it seemed to me anyway to be in very magisterial language – but I don't know if you'll get many theologians to say that this was an infallible statement. Cardinal Ratzinger, as he was then, spoke sometime shortly after *Ordinatio sacerdo-*

talis and he had no doubt that it was infallible teaching because it came from the ordinary magisterium of the church. But that did not find favour with many theologians. And this is why what the prefect has identified seems to me to be something that is very important for future consideration.

Yes, the prefect says: this is common doctrine but still lacks clarity on the modality of recognising when one may be able to say about a particular doctrine that it is infallibly guaranteed by the universal ordinary magisterium. Now I am not saying that there is a simple answer. All I am saying is that this is something that requires deep reflection.

Now, the prefect also wonders about the implementation of collegiality. Perhaps in the future, other instances of the bishops' collegial action such as the synod of bishops will have a role in helping to identify such teaching of the ordinary universal magisterium. Yes, I see that but what is a synod? A synod is a meeting of about 200 bishops. They come from different episcopal conferences. Do all the bishops in the episcopal conference agree with what the delegate or what the representative is going to say? Will he bring along the voting on the various different aspects of whatever it may be so that the synod will know how things stand in the episcopal conference? All I am saying and I am not trying to block anything, is, how would the synod operate this kind of collegial action? Quite certainly there is no difficulty about an ecumenical council where all the bishops are present.

Now I know it has been a long day and I think it is about time that I stopped talking. One of the difficulties is that when you see a former professor standing up with notes you can be worried. If you see him standing up without notes, you can give up! I am very grateful to you for listening to me so patiently. I do once again wish to express my deep gratitude for all that has been done for me on this day.

Encounter Jesus now: homily at vespers

ARCHBISHOP DIARMUID MARTIN

WITH THIS LITURGICAL ACT, we move from our moment of celebration right into the heart of the lenten message. On the first Sunday of Lent, the church recalls Jesus being driven by the Spirit into the wilderness and being tempted by Satan and how Jesus begins his mission with an urgent call to repentance.

Mark provides no details of the temptation, except to stress that it was by Satan. Jesus is led by the Spirit into the wilderness where his ministry appears in the form of a trial of strength between his saving message and the powers of evil. That trial of strength continues in our hearts and in our world today. The primary weapon that we can use in this conflict is the same one as used by Jesus: abandonment in trust to his Father, knowing that his loving care will look after us, just as the angels cared for Jesus.

In Lent through our prayers, penance and acts of charity we recognise our own fragility. We recognise the fragility of our origins 'remember you are dust' and the fragility of our life which will end. We recognise the fragilities which we cover with our arrogance and self-seeking. We recognise the fragility of the human endeavour which despite enormous scientific and social progress has not been able to root out violence and cruelty, hunger or deprivation. Where do we turn?

The Lord knows our fragility. He invites us to abandon ourselves and place our trust entirely in his loving kindness. He calls us to abandon the masks of false security, whether they be personal affirmation and aggrandisement, or social convention or following the fashions of the day or our own addictions and cravings. Conversation means moving away from external securities and returning totally to a dependence on the things of God.

After the temptation, after experiencing in the form of temptation the conflict between the Son of God and Satan, Jesus begins his ministry of proclaiming the Gospel of God. Once again the summary given by Mark is scarce in detail, yet precisely because of the scarcity of detail it is quite clear and focussed. Jesus announces that the time has come; that the time of expectation of preparation is over. His hearers will have quickly recognised that Jesus is presenting himself as quite different from any prophet of the past. Jesus' message is not just a teaching about the kingdom but an announcement that the kingdom was present in his person.

The scarcity of detail accentuates the urgency that permeates this proclamation and the consequent call to repentance. The call is urgent. The answer to the call is not a protracted period of personal discernment much less negotiation. The answer is to recognise the radical newness of Jesus. Jesus and his message are so radically new that the only response is to shed what belongs to the old order of our lives, to abandon all our old ways and habits and commit ourselves fully to this new master.

In this sense the stress of Mark is not on the content of the message but on the urgency that is placed on responding to the call of Jesus. The church can very easily lose that sense of urgency in its preaching and in its ministry. We have to fight against the temptation of acquiescence and the tempta-tion of turning the church and religion into a comfort zone. The Word of God is always a call to be alert. The church can easily acquiesce in its posi-tion of presence and status in society and has loose the dynamism of being a missionary church.

Many in our times never find their way to Jesus because they acquiesce in superficiality or in a faith in the possibilities of human efforts on their own. Many have lost any sense of the need of salvation because we live as if salvation was something that we owned rather than recognising that salva-tion is a gift, an invitation by a God who is love.

It is only by breaking away from convention and habit that we can begin to recognise our dependence and fragility. But recognising our dependence on God is not something which paralyses or demeans our human potential. It frees us to take the risk of being counter-cultural, of seeing human realities in their depth, of discovering faith in the space of our own freedom.

Encountering Jesus as the revelation of God's love is an experience which transforms us. When we experience the love of God as invitation we are called up into the very interior of life of God, the love for the Father for the Son. We are called to repent of our selfishness and self-centredness through being taken up into the self-giving, sacrificial, saving love of God revealed in Jesus. Then we are freed to bring that Good News of God into the world with the newness and urgency it entails. We are freed to transform self-giving into love, both the norm of our life and the norm of social interaction in a world where the powers of Satan and evil still sow the seeds of hatred, violence and exclusion.

Mary abandoned herself to God's call and set out on her path of life 'according to God's Word' – which is the motto of Cardinal Connell – pondering the Word in her heart day by day and being alongside her Son, with fidelity and trust, as the mystery of his life death and resurrection unfolded according to God's plan. May she be our model as we embark on our Lenten path of renewal and conversation.

Reflections on the brokenness of the Irish church

ANDREW G. McGRADY

FROM PALM SUNDAY TO GOOD FRIDAY

MY FIRST ENCOUNTER WITH Cardinal Desmond Connell was when, as an undergraduate student of religious education in Dublin in 1969, I was enrolled in his lectures on philosophy. He taught us philosophical theology including the five proofs for the existence of God. I was fascinated by his scholarly approach, and my fellow students and I all took it for granted that the analytical tradition of the church, and the manner in which faith built on reason and was reasonable, provided a firm foundation for our role with Irish society. In the 1960s and 70s the church in Ireland was at its zenith. Catholicism gave meaning to personal life and coherence to a republic which was defined by its faithfulness to Catholicism The bishops were influential and respected leaders, the seminaries and noviciates were full, the education and health care systems were largely administered by the church. It was said that if you threw a penny into the air in O'Connell Street it would land on the head of a priest or a religious brother or sister. The churches were full not only for Sunday Mass but also for devotions such as Benediction. There was a close correspondence between government social policy and the teaching of the church. The Second Vatican Council had just ended. True, the archbishop of Dublin, John Charles McQuaid, had returned from Rome with the reported comment that nothing that had happened would disturb the simple faith of the Irish people, but it would not be true to say that the church in Ireland was static. The same John Charles McQuaid had sent some of his priests to study mass media, an initiative which directly influenced the development of the RTE *Radharc* series (which is still running) and he had been a major influence in the establishment of the Catholic Communications Institute of Ireland which included the Communications Centre and its state of the art television studios in Booterstown. There were numerous educational initiatives such as the opening of Saint Patrick's College, Maynooth, to lay students, the founding of Mater Dei Institute as a centre for catechetics in Dublin, the establishment of the Institute for Adult Religious Education in Mount Oliver near Dundalk, and the establishment of the Centre for Pastoral Liturgy at Saint Anne's in Portarlington. As a young graduate of Mater Dei Institute I had the privilege of working with staff of the Communications Centre who travelled to every diocese in the country providing courses on preaching, media education and television interviewing techniques. So many initiatives for sharing the Gospel showed such promise. These were exciting times and there was a strong sense that everything was possible for the Irish church immediately after the Second Vatican Council. The church in Ireland was not static in those days forty years ago, but it was too certain, complacent and over confident about its rightful place in society.

Thus almost forty years later, in 2006, the situation concerning the Catholic church in Ireland has changed utterly. Our dominant experience today is one of brokenness. There can be little doubt that the most public moment in the brokenness of the Irish church relates to the issue of sexual abuse and the perceived response of the leaders of the church to this situation. I emphasise 'perceived' response because I do not believe that our leaders acted dishonestly or without integrity. But they have been perceived as placing institutional maintenance ahead of a truly open and honest response and, in a media-dominated public space, what matters is what is perceived. Sex abuse has hit the Irish church like a tsunami. The earthquake at its source was largely unwitnessed, it took place deep below the surface and people went about their daily lives unaware of the impending catastrophe. But it did surface and the tidal wave it created has destroyed so much in its path – people's lives and shared common beliefs. Confidence, certainty and status have been undermined and many stand by in shock and disbelief.

AT THE FOOT OF THE CROSS STOOD HIS MOTHER MARY

The dominant image in my mind is that of the moment in which the body of the crucified Jesus was taken from the cross and laid in the arms of his mother Mary who was supported in her grief by the apostle John, Mary the wife of Clopas and Mary of Magdala (Jn 19:25–26). The followers of Jesus had entered Jerusalem in triumph and jubilation on Palm Sunday. Those inside the city had welcomed him by crying out 'blessings on him who comes in the name of the Lord' (Ps 118:26 and Lk 19:38). The disciples had hoped that Jesus would be 'the one to set Israel free' (Lk 24:21). Days later those same followers had deserted or denied Jesus, the citizens of Jerusalem had changed their cry to 'Crucify him, crucify him!' (Lk 23:20) and Jesus had been executed as a common criminal outside the walls of the city that he had so recently entered in triumph.

Of course, the radical change in the position of the Irish church in Irish society is not just due to the tsunami of sexual abuse. This occurred as an earthquake deep beneath the surface, hidden from view. But the surface of the ocean had already been disturbed by the winds of increasing economic prosperity, individualism, apathy and secularism – Irish-style. Thus the signs reflecting the shift from a religious public culture to a secular individualistic culture were already well established – the end of large numbers of vocations to the ministerial priesthood and religious life, falling participation in eucharistic liturgies and other sacramental celebrations, the declining interest among those still active in the Sunday liturgy in taking part in lay liturgical ministry, and the alienation and 'resignation' of many women and urban young adults from the institutional life of the church. Even before the tsunami, the church failed to enter into a fruitful dialogue with the newly emerging Irish society and identities. It seemed paralysed by the impact of 'religionism' on the sectarian conflict in Northern Ireland and, while relationships and dialogue between leaders of the church and other Christian leaders on the island of Ireland were well conducted, such ecumenical vision did not filter down to the grassroots of church membership. As a result people became aware that religious loyalties could contribute in a destructive rather than constructive manner to peace and social cohesion. In daily life generally, people were moving to a 'cultural Catholicism' anyway, in which they followed their own conscience, particularly in areas of sexual morality, rather than obeying the teaching of the church. The authority of the church was being eroded by its perceived intransigence and growing irrelevance. But these worrying storms on the surface were not of the same order of magnitude as when the tsunami of sexual abuse ruptured the ocean surface. There is no aspect of the life of the Irish Catholic church that has not been reached by the resultant tidal wave. Many people have lost confidence in the institutional expression of the church. Cardinals, bishops, priests, religious, and lay people share in this brokenness, hurt and deep shock. Many have been vilified, perhaps some with justification, but many unfairly. But all of us in the Irish church must accept some responsibility for the brokenness and failure of the institution. Now, as never before, is a time for all members of the church to speak together with love rather than resentment.

GRIEVING, REMEMBERING AND DISCERNING

It is of course possible to find hope in the core Christian belief that 'Christ has died, Christ is risen, Christ will come again' and that the church is going through a process of purification and will re-emerge as a smaller, stronger, more faithful, vibrant church. Be that as it may, now is not the time to talk of a 'resurrected church'. I have felt for many years that our celebration of the *New order of Christian funerals* places too strong an emphasis on the hope of the resurrection and does not place sufficient emphasis on accompanying those who grieve in their experience of deep sorrow. The Irish church is grieving and is currently in shock. It is too soon to talk of resurrection. The body of Jesus hangs dead on the cross; his mortal remains are being removed from the cross and placed in the grieving arms of his mother and closest family. We are moving his body to lay it in the tomb. He has not yet 'descended to the dead'; Easter Sunday has not yet dawned. It is still days off. In the late 1960s, in popular psychology, Elisabeth Kubler-Ross identified five stages of grief – denial, anger, bargaining, depression, and finally acceptance. In its grief the Irish church is still in the early stages and is a long way from the final stage of acceptance.

One of the things that those who grieve do to put words on their sorrow is to remember. They re-tell, again and again, the narrative of the death of their loved one. It is as if some release from shock comes from such re-telling. The events surrounding death are so unfathomable that it is only by repeating them, and repeating them again and again, that the reality that all is changed begins to be glimpsed (if not yet fully accepted). Once the immediate events begin to be accepted other narratives from the life of the loved one who has died begin to be voiced. There is a process of remembering the life that was shared with the deceased loved one, a process which gradually develops into a re-membering of relationships for a continuing life in which that loved one is present in a different way. Such a time of remembering and re-membering is crucial to those who grieve. It must not be suppressed, denied or too quickly brought to closure. Similarly those who grieve are not able to hear rational, intellectual argument. I believe that the Irish church is still in these early stages of grief. Yes, Easter Sunday will dawn – but not yet. Now is the time for remembering and re-membering; now is a time for reflection and discernment.

THIS IS MY BODY, BROKEN FOR YOU

There comes a point in the storytelling of those who are grieving when they relate their personal sorrow to a wider, transcendent framework. They talk about the death of their loved one as 'being God's will', of the loved one's pain and sickness as 'being over', of their being in a 'better place', and of 'this being part of God's plan' . . . So too as we grieve the broken body of the Irish church we begin to tell other stories that transcend the present moment. The most important of these stories relates to the belief that that which has been broken is not just a human institution but also the very body of Christ and to the belief that such brokenness can be redemptive.

A SPIRITUAL HUNGER

What has been taken down from the cross is a particular historical, cultural and institutional expression of the Irish Catholic church. It is people's confidence and respect for this institutional expression, not their search for God, which has died. People are grieving because they invested so much relating to their beliefs and values on that institutional expression and they feel betrayed and shocked. Many priests feel uneasy in their role; many parents feel that they have been undermined in the passing on of authentic values to their children; many teachers find it difficult to present the teachings of the church to a younger generation who stare at them with incredulity. But as we engage in a fuller process of remembering and re-telling, it is immediately apparent that there are other stories being told during this period of grieving. At parish level, individual priests are generally highly respected and their ministry is valued. Most people acknowledge a positive pastoral experience of priests at funerals and marriages. In general, people also report a positive experience for celebrations of first communion and confirmation. Many parishes are creative in their celebration of the liturgy.

As confidence in, and affiliation with, the institutional church declines, a deep spiritual hunger is emerging. This is evidenced in so many ways, all of which are expressions of displacement. The 'rootlessness', characteristic of the post-modern condition, manifests itself by a sense that the links between the present and the past and the present and the future have been severed. It is hard to tell stories of transcendence when there is little sense of history, a loss of memory, or a retreat from community. The moral certainty of former times has been replaced by a personal internal pluralism: people simultaneously inhabit many cultures and adopt diverse identities in different contexts. There is a loss of a sense of authority. The sources of authority are no longer external but internal, and the criterion for validity is no longer the credibility of the external authoritative source but the criterion of personal experience. The shift from institutional religious affiliation to a more individual, *à la carte* spirituality has led to a separation of the religious, the moral and the spiritual dimensions of life.

Different patterns of religiosity are increasingly evident for men and women. Sociologically, the Irish situation is increasingly like that of the rest of Europe, with many people 'believing without belonging'.

CHURCH AND COMMUNITY

The pillars of Irish society have traditionally been the parish, the home and the school. As these have changed radically, so too has the sense of community. In the past (especially in rural contexts) there was an overlap between the parish and the local community. This relationship is under strain. There are a number of reasons for this. The first is economic. Despite almost full employment, rising incomes and relatively low levels of direct personal taxation, the quality of family life is in decline. The high price of property in the cities has led to the rapid expansion of the commuter belt into rural areas. Most families cannot survive on a single income. Thus both spouses tend to work outside the home and need to commute long distances to work. It is the 'under fives' who are paying the price for the Celtic tiger. They are away from their family homes for up to twelve hours a day; their experience of a stable, nurturing home is disrupted. For many families, the evenings and weekends are about survival rather than engagement with the local community or parish liturgy.

The second factor is of course social. The sociology of the family unit is changing. The traditional pattern of two parents, married to each other, establishing a home with children to which they have given birth, watched over and supported by grandparents, is fast disappearing. Further, local communities are experiencing inward migration as part of the globalisation of Ireland. Such inward migration is an economic necessity and has the potential to enrich Irish society, but it raises vital questions about identity, culture and social cohesion.

The final factor of importance is the school. In the past there was a strong link between the school, the church and the local community particularly at primary level and at secondary level in rural areas. The strength of this link is also weakening, and the role of the church in the administration of the education system is visibly changing. The decline in numbers of priests and the religiously professed working in schools has led to the emergence of new trustee structures, issues concerning leadership succession and the definition of the ethos, or characteristic spirit, of the Catholic school. Articulating what is distinctive about the Catholic school is a matter of priority, but it is clear that we have moved from a position in which the schooling system in the Republic was largely a Catholic system to a position in which, as diversity of educational provision increases, Catholic schools are becoming just one option among others. The downside of this is to weaken the intimate connection between the Catholic school and the local community. Increased parental choice (which is a constitutional right) has resulted in a shift away from denominational schools. The fastest growing sector at primary level is the 'educate together' sector. Also, in 2005 the Vocational Education Committee (VEC) sector opened its first national school. Most newly established schools are not under the patronage of the church – parents are choosing a different route. The *gael scoileanna* are also growing in number and they too incarnate a multi-denominational ethos. There are high levels of parental satisfaction with existing Catholic national schools, but these schools too are challenged to respond to increasing pupil diversity and changing parental expectations. Further, young primary school teachers reflect the general changes in Irish culture concerning attitudes towards religion and personal religiosity. The issue of sacramental preparation is becoming problematic, and there are increasing calls for a state multi-faith syllabus for religious education at primary level.

At post-primary level the number of Catholic voluntary secondary schools is declining and very few schools are being established in this sector. The preferred model of Department of Education and Science for new post-primary schools is that of community and comprehensive schools and colleges. While parents are generally not antagonistic towards the ethos of Catholic schools, the majority select such schools for other reasons than the faith development they provide.

I recently carried out research with three and a half thousand parents who had enrolled their children in seventy-nine Catholic voluntary secondary schools. This research indicated that what such parents value most is the extent to which the school caters to the full range of interests and abilities of their child and the approach to discipline adopted by the school. Parents nostalgically accept the religious, spiritual and moral dimensions of the curriculum of the Catholic school and expect their children to participate in the religious education provided. But they expect their child to study the broad religious heritage of humankind in an open and appreciative manner. One in three parents who enrolled their child in Catholic voluntary secondary schools did not wish the school to engage in faith formation. Further, a majority of parents did not accept that, when approaching the teaching of controversial moral and social issues, the school should exclusively favour the teaching of the Catholic church (only 31% supported favouring the stance of the church). When asked about the future role of the church in post-primary education, only 46% of these parents who had enrolled their child in a Catholic school considered that the church should continue to have a prominent role; 42% considered that the church should have a reduced role; and 12% thought that the church should have no future role. The research also strongly indicated that the most important consideration influencing the effectiveness of the religious education provided by the school was the extent to which parents themselves were perceived by their children as being supportive of, and valuing, the faith formation activities of the school. Partnership with parents is thus the key to the work of the school in the area of faith formation and development.

EVANGELISATION AND THE FACE OF JESUS

It is too early to talk about a resurrection for the Irish church, and simplistic suggestions concerning a way forward are not helpful. As we continue in a state of shock and mourning, it is however healing to begin to tell other stories. The story we should begin to tell is not the story of the death of a particular historical, cultural institutional expression of church, but the story of the life, death and resurrection of Jesus who is Lord and

Christ. And as we look to the wider community of the Catholic church we see that this is the story being told. The late Pope John Paul II placed a strong emphasis on proclaiming the face of Jesus at the start of the new millennium. The church at the local level is increasingly challenged to offer an invitation to faith rather than presuming that such faith is already present. This invitation is primarily one to faith in Jesus and to a response of discipleship. It is Christ that we must proclaim; it is a personal relationship with God in Christ that we must offer. We do this in the firm conviction that it is Jesus who reveals the fullness of what it is to be human; it is he who guides our search for meaning. It is through conversion to him that the individual and wider Irish culture can be transformed. This was the hope of John Paul II at the start of the third millennium:

> 'Your face, O Lord, I seek' (Ps 27:8). The ancient longing of the psalmist could receive no fulfillment greater and more surprising than the contemplation of the face of Christ. God has truly blessed us in him and has made 'his face to shine upon us' (Ps 67:1). At the same time, God and man that he is, he reveals to us also the true face of man, 'fully revealing man to man himself' . . . Jesus is 'the new man' (cf. Eph 4:24; Col 3:10) who calls redeemed humanity to share in his divine life. The mystery of the Incarnation lays the foundations for an anthropology which, reaching beyond its own limitations and contradictions, moves towards God himself, indeed towards the goal of 'divinization'. [1]

This is the task of a new evangelisation.

BE GOOD NEWS: EVANGELISATION AND LOVING SERVICE

I believe that the most promising current development in the Irish Catholic Church is the process leading to the issuing of a National Catechetical Directory. During 2006 a draft, an unpublished version of

---

[1]   John Paul II, *Novo millennio ineunte*, 23.

this, *Be Good News,* has been circulated for consultation. This draft rightly argues that evangelisation is central to the life of the church and is the responsibility of all. In its interaction with Irish people and Irish society in the past, the church presumed the existence of a firm faith. Today it must begin from a different starting point – that of a new evangelisation, which invites rather than presumes faith. Such evangelisation is to be regarded as a life-long process. Effective evangelisation is seen to require a joint, coordinated effort of the family, the parish and the school. But the most important aspect of the vision of the draft National Catechetical Directory may be its title – *Be Good News.* Evangelisation is not seen simply as message – it is something that is to be lived both individually and as a church community. We are to evangelise not just by what we say but by what we do and who we are.

It is hoped that, following the results of consultation, the Irish Episcopal Conference will approve a final version of the National Catechetical Directory in the short to medium term. This would be a welcome development. Many local churches produced their National Catechetical Directory thirty years ago, and some are on their second edition. Such a final version of the directory will hopefully place a strong emphasis on the three key areas for evangelisation – adult faith development, the faith formation of children and adolescents in the home, the primary school and the post-primary school and the evangelisation that occurs by reaching out to all in love. A focus on the foundational nature of adult evangelisation would be welcome especially since a systematic approach to this area has been somewhat absent in Ireland in the past. Adult faith formation has generally been a neglected area. Similarly an emphasis on evangelisation, faith formation and faith development as being the shared work of the home, the school and the parish working collaboratively in a manner which respects the distinct and unique contribution of each partner would provide an important synthesis and foundation for future structures.

An emphasis upon evangelisation through loving action as well as words is an important emerging theme in the teaching of Pope Benedict XVI. In his previous work as cardinal, the present pope was a champion of his predecessor's call for a new evangelisation of Europe. Since he became pope, Benedict has explicitly linked the themes of new evangelisation and love, especially in his first encyclical *Deus caritas est* – 'I wish in my first encyclical to speak of the love which God lavishes upon us and which we in turn must share with others' (no. 1). The pope insists that 'every Christian community is called . . . to make known God, who is Love'.[2] Reflecting on the words of the First Letter of Saint John, 'We have come to believe in God's love,'[3] he emphasises that 'in these words the Christian can express the fundamental decision of his life. Being Christian is not the result of an ethical choice or a lofty idea, but the encounter with an event, a person, which gives life a new horizon and a decisive direction.'[4] For Benedict a commitment to love not only forms the basis of individual discipleship but is the work of the evangelising community that is the church. He synthesises his teaching as follows:

> The entire activity of the church is an expression of a love that seeks the integral good of man: it seeks his evangelization through Word and Sacrament, an undertaking that is often heroic in the way it is acted out in history; and it seeks to promote man in the various arenas of life and human activity. Love is therefore the service that the church carries out in order to attend constantly to man's sufferings and his needs, including material needs.[5]

If the final, approved version of a National Catechetical Directory follows the approach taken in *Be Good News*, and is responsive to the emphasis of the present pope on evangelisation through loving service, it would have important strategic and resource implications for the Irish church – at a time when financial resources are seriously depleted. It would present the church with a *kairos* moment. For the first time in recent

2 Pope Benedict XVI, *Charity, the soul of mission.* Message for World Mission Sunday 2006, no. 2.
3 1 Jn 4:16.
4 Pope Benedict XVI, *Deus caritas est*, 1.
5 Ibid., 19.

decades the church would have the basis for a pastoral plan. Responding to this moment will require discernment, effective, imaginative and creative leadership and consensus building. Never before has the Irish church had at its disposal so many theologically literate and pastorally qualified lay people ready to share in its ministry. Rarely have all the people of God been so challenged to connect 'faith and life' and 'faith and culture'. Collaborative approaches to ministry are not an option but a necessity. The involvement of lay people in paid ministry has obvious financial implications that are not easily addressed. Consensus building also requires a process of consultation and listening through which a shared vision can be articulated and, of which, all members of the people of God, be they bishops, priests, religious or lay people, be they male or female, be they young or old, can take ownership. The Irish church has never held a national synod involving representatives of all its members. Many believe that such a synod would make a distinctive and pivotal contribution. Further, such new evangelisation must be distinctively Irish. We know from the previous phases of evangelisation from the time of Saint Patrick that effective evangelisation must dialogue with the deep and distinctive spirituality of the Irish which is characterised by an affective connectedness with the mystery and cycles of the created order. Faith for the Irish is primarily a felt response. The Irish will not be re-evangelised by theological propositions but by a continuous linkage of the mystery at the heart of their experience with the meta-narrative of the paschal mystery of Christ. If the new evangelisation of individuals and of Irish society is to be effective it must be planted in such soil.

CONCLUSION

Recently, Pope Benedict noted that 'evangelizing action must walk the road Christ himself walked, a way of poverty and obedience, of service and self-sacrifice even to death, a death from which he emerged victorious. Yes! The church is called to serve the humanity of our time by trusting in Jesus alone, by allowing herself to be illumined by his Word and imitating him in the generous gift of herself to his brethren.'[6] These words ring true for the Irish church in the broken situation it finds itself in today. The immediate challenge is not to deny our brokenness or grief, but by a process of reflection and discernment, to interpret such brokenness through the paradigm of the brokenness of Jesus and, by drawing on this experience, to become an evangelising community for a broken world. The person who successfully negotiates a path through the grieving process emerges as a stronger, humbler, more compassionate person. Such a person does not deny what has happened but integrates it into a richer, more grounded faith. They know that there is no going back to a past that has died. The person who never successfully negotiates a path through the grieving process remains entombed in sorrow, buried in the past, unable to 'look for the living among the dead' (Lk 24:5). Our grieving is a time for linking our experience of brokenness as church with the crucifixion of Jesus; in this way we will discern the way to authentically bear witness to a God who is love, and proclaim the presence of the risen Lord and Christ to the new Ireland and the new Irish of today.

---

6 Benedict XVI, *Address on the occasion of the 40th anniversary of the conciliar decree* 'Ad gentes'. Rome, 11 March 2006.

The spirituality of study

THOMAS G. CASEY SJ

TIPS ABOUT STUDY SKILLS and advice on how to prepare for examinations are always welcome. It helps to learn how to schedule time, write papers, and face difficult test questions. But Christians and Catholics rarely step back and ponder what study means in a deeper context. How does it fit into our lives of faith? Although this reflective exercise is not as immediately practical as learning better study techniques, it is immensely valuable. To be good Christians and effective apostles, we must value the mind and treasure wisdom.

Many priests, religious and lay people grapple with the problem of how to integrate study into religious and priestly life. Ideally, seminarians view study as a useful preparation for ministry. But even this stance is not as positive as it sounds, for they regard study as only a prelude to the real substance of life and work. They fail to see that study can be something substantial and valuable in itself. In practice, they often find it difficult to value study even as something useful; they often view it in less positive and sanguine terms. For instance, when they find themselves wading through courses that are particularly monotonous or uninspiring, they can be tempted to regard study as a necessary evil.

Even though most religious, priests and lay people are not engaged in full-time study, their lives can be enriched if they learn to re-envisage study. It makes a big difference if we can look on study as something that enhances rather than diminishes, as something that is a gift rather than a burden. Granted, most of us are not going to spend our lives engaged in full-time study, though it would be heartening if more Christians seriously considered the intellectual calling. But even if we do not envisage giving a substantial amount of time and energy to study, we should nevertheless give quality-time to study. In order to meet the challenges of our world, we have got to use our God-given gift of intelligence. We need to exercise it, nourish it and develop it.

After all, study is a focus for practically all of us at some time or other. Not just during school and formal education, but also in the course of adult life when we do renewal courses, training workshops or take study sabbaticals. Indeed, the questions raised by people and events on a daily basis regularly compel us to reflect and ponder more deeply on our faith, on the big questions of life. It is a fact that study is part of our lives. How can we make it a fruitful experience? How can we weave study into the fabric of our lives and service?

The classic work on the spirituality of study is *The intellectual life: its spirit, conditions, methods* by the French Dominican A.G. Sertillanges (1863–1948), originally published in French in 1920.[1] Sertillanges' beautifully written book is a radiant gem that should top every student's must-read list. It is a learned, passionate book of marvellous depth that highlights the sacred nature of the call to study. Above all it is eminently practical, offering a wealth of insights about how to go about the business of studying in the midst of our daily lives.

Given that Sertillanges' book is so outstanding, is there anything new worth saying? Yes. First of all, we are living in a new cultural context with new challenges. Secondly, the explicit command of Jesus to develop our minds is a command that is rarely adverted to, but certainly needs to be clearly proclaimed. Thirdly, the Ignatian tradition offers a rich perspective on the importance of desire, something essential to the life of study. And finally, since Sertillanges' book has been neglected for too long, this article is an invitation to return to his study that is too good to be forgotten or missed.

SPIRITUALITY AND STUDY

St Ignatius of Loyola stresses the centrality of desire in spirituality. In his *Spiritual exercises*, Ignatius echoes the question of Jesus in John's Gospel,

---

1   A.G. Sertillanges, *The intellectual life: its spirit, conditions, methods*, trans. M. Ryan (Washington DC, 1998).

'What do you desire?' (Jn 1: 38). He continually invites the exercitant to get in touch with his or her desires. Desire is fundamental to spirituality, because spirituality is about getting in touch with our desires, tapping their energy, and channelling these desires toward God.

Today there is a crying desire for justice around the world. There is also a less obvious yet no less burning hunger for truth. As human beings we seek the full truth about ourselves and everything else. Evidence of this immense thirst for truth can be found in innumerable places, not only in the realms of religion or philosophy. Let's take two examples, one from art and another from literature.

In 1897 Paul Gauguin, who had moved to Tahiti some years beforehand, set to work on a famous painting that he intended as a spiritual testament. The painting, widely regarded as his masterpiece, now hangs in the Boston Museum of Fine Arts. The painting's title articulates the central truth-driven questions that perennially haunt us: 'Where do we come from? What are we? Where are we going?' Interestingly, Gauguin first heard these questions from the mouth of Bishop Dupanloup, who taught the future artist when he was a teenage student at the junior seminary in Orléans. Although Gauguin later rejected the Catholic faith, he never forgot these fundamental questions that he learned from Bishop Dupanloup.

These are the questions that all great art is concerned with. They are also the core questions that every human being is challenged to face over the course of a lifetime. Although Gauguin had left behind a successful business career in Paris and taken up a simpler, more elemental existence in the Polynesian Islands, he was still grappling with these basic questions to the end of his life.

The second example comes from the fiction of the leading Irish writer James Joyce, another great artist who was indebted to the Catholic faith against which he rebelled. Joyce, like Cardinal Connell, was a pupil at Belvedere College. Before moving to Belvedere, Joyce had attended Clongowes Wood College, the Jesuit boarding school in Kildare. Joyce evokes the desire for a full and complete possession of the truth in a scene from the school-life of Stephen Dedalus. The young protagonist of *A portrait of the artist as a young man* is sitting in the study hall of Clongowes Wood College, trying to come to grips with all the places and names in his geography book: 'They were all in different countries and the countries were in continents and the continents were in the world and the world was in the universe . . . What was after the universe?'[2]

Study is an activity of the mind that seeks the truth about a particular subject. The mind explores and examines a discipline with a view to transforming the unknown into the known, in order to throw light on what was previously dark. Study seeks to make the object of study intelligible. The spirituality of study is faithful to the depth of Paul Gauguin's questions, seeking the truth about our beginnings, identity, and final destination. The spirituality of study is never satisfied with half-measures, posing questions as daring as that of Stephen Dedalus: 'what comes after the universe?' The spirituality of study is about channelling our desires in the direction of knowledge and truth. It is about giving us a sense of how and where study fits into our lives as Christians; it is about integrating study into our lives so that it is not divorced from our faith but instead acts as a gathering force and focus for our Christian commitment.

OBSTACLES

The social and personal obstacles to a spirituality of study are so pervasive that we do not always notice them. They seem as natural as the air we breathe or as the water surrounding a fish. Here are two examples of barriers to serious study: first of all, the excess of information in our culture, and secondly the consequences of the banishment of religion from public life.

Western societies are flooded with information: on the worldwide web, cell phones, TV and elsewhere. The volume of information is so great that it cannot be assimilated; it is so disjointed that its connection with any framework of meaning is often accidental, and usually tenuous. This vast tangle of information does not always enrich our lives; it often destabilises

2   J. Joyce, *A portrait of the artist as a young man*, ed. S. Deane (London, 1992), pp 12–13.

them. The way we receive this information does not invite us to ponder issues in a thoughtful and reflective way. For instance, the simplicity of text-messaging on a cell phone does not facilitate the complex discussion of political issues; the headlines in a tabloid newspaper furnish us with easily digestible and often misleading soundbites. We are urged to stick labels on issues and people, and to treat complex questions in a brief and condensed way. We are encouraged to respond emotionally rather than with our reason. In other words, the less thinking we do the better. And in any case, we have little time to dwell on anything, since our attention is quickly distracted by something new. These technologies of social and personal communication militate against the persistence and tenacity that wise and intelligent Christianity demands. How can we bathe ourselves in silence if we hear constant noise? How can we be receptive to the light of God if our attention is distracted by the flickering light of TV screens and ringing cell-phones?

Secondly, let us consider some of the effects of the relegation of religion to the private sphere. The culture of western Europe likes to define itself by secular values, and does not like to acknowledge the importance of Christianity in its historical development and present identity. Many Christians have internalised western culture's belief that faith belongs to the private and subjective sphere, and they are inclined to share the assumption that it has little to offer in the public forum. And so they have retreated from public debate and marginalised themselves to a private space. Faith is often seen as a matter of feeling. There is a tendency to reduce religion to sentimentality, to prioritise above all a culture of feeling and experience, and reject a culture of reason and tradition. The claims of faith have been battered so relentlessly by certain currents of thought that believers fear their faith may not be rationally defensible at all. Christians themselves are not sure how much their faith is supported by reason, how true it really is. Witness the success of *The Da Vinci code*, the main argument of which is that Mary Magdalene had a daughter by Jesus whose descendants survive until this day in France. This thriller starts with a page entitled 'fact,' suggesting that much of what follows is not fictional, and that the Catholic church is implicated in a centuries-long cover-up of the truth.

Because of the confinement of faith to the private realm, many Christians do not realise that it is possible to integrate Christianity and law, that business can be studied from a Christian perspective, that the healing miracles of Jesus can speak to the world of medicine. We are living in a western-dominated world culture that does not associate Christianity with life-enhancing wisdom or penetrating intelligence. These doubts have infected believers as well. This means that we have to make a conscious and deep-rooted choice to enrich our Christian minds. But this difficult cultural situation is also an invitation to us to be courageous. We need to be 'as wise as serpents,' in other words we need to study, and we need to be 'as innocent as doves' (Mt 10:16); in other words we need to lead lives of transparent goodness, with a deep spirituality.

OBEYING A FUNDAMENTAL COMMANDMENT

Serving God through our intellects is not simply an optional extra in Christianity. It is not up to our discretion. It is not something we can decide to embrace or discard at our pleasure. Loving God with our minds is an essential and indispensable aspect of faith.

There is a surprising ignorance about the importance of study among Christians. Many Catholics and Christians do not realise that Jesus himself commands us to love God with our minds and intelligence. It is not as if Jesus transmitted this commandment in a hidden or an indirect way. In order to impart this vital message, he did not use metaphors, he did not recite parables. In fact he spelled out this commandment as clearly and unambiguously as possible. Perhaps because this commandment is so obvious, it is often so overlooked. Or maybe it is a matter of selective blindness: precisely because we do not expect God to command us to love him with our minds, we do not even realize that he asks us to do so.

This particular commandment is not a minor or unimportant one. On the contrary, it has absolute priority, because it is the first and most important commandment of all.

Hearing that Jesus had silenced the Sadducees, the Pharisees got together. One of them, an expert in the law, tested him with this question: 'Teacher, which is the greatest commandment in the Law?' Jesus replied: '"Love the Lord your God with all your heart and with all your soul and with all your mind." This is the first and greatest commandment' (Mt 22: 34–38).

Many Christians have heard this commandment proclaimed innumerable times. Yet how many of us have noticed the word 'mind'? How many of us have thought about its meaning? How many of us have come to see that God commands us to love him not only with all our hearts and all our souls, but also with all our minds (intellectually)? Jesus is clearly telling us that we cannot genuinely love God without loving him intellectually as well.

Christian neglect of the mind is rarely a matter of deliberate choice or wilful malice. It is most often down to unintentional ignorance. Many of us are not even aware that the failure to love God with our whole minds is a form of disobedience. Generally, the failure to do something good is less blameworthy than the deliberate choice of something evil. All these factors – unintentional ignorance, lack of knowledge and omission – render our transgression of this commandment significantly less culpable.

Nevertheless, the failure to fulfill this commandment wounds us, and undermines our service to others. To neglect the mind, to fail to nurture this talent God has given us, is not merely regrettable and unfortunate. There is something more serious at issue here, since it is potentially catastrophic in its consequences. These consequences are both personal and social in nature. On a personal level, if we neglect to exercise the mind, our intellects become flabby and complacent. We end up focusing on what is less intellectually demanding, things like sex, the body, money, clothes, gadgets. All of these physical and material things promise immediate gratification, whereas the intellect doesn't. At the same time, our belief in a world beyond the senses diminishes. When we fill our minds only with what we can see, hear, touch, taste and smell, then the empirical world becomes the sum and summit of reality for us. When we stop thinking about values, principles, the soul, God, and immortality, these vital and invisible realities begin to seem less real.

On the social level, the neglect of the life of the mind leads to a church that is unable to speak intelligently about its faith. It becomes afraid of witnessing to its faith; it feels inadequate and inferior when non-Christians engage it in discussion. The Christian faith loses its intellectual cutting-edge as a result. Believers feel they have nothing constructive to offer in debates about delicate ethical issues or the future of society. The wider culture soon begins to suspect Christianity may be something irrational. It becomes all too easy to dismiss a belief system which seems unworthy of intelligent and reflective human beings. This neglect of the life of the mind is all the more lamentable because we possess such a wonderful intellectual heritage as Catholics and as Christians.

THE IMPORTANCE OF DESIRE

Paradoxically, when it comes to the life of the mind, once the presence of normal intelligence is presumed, the most important factor is not intelligence itself: the crucial element is the will. A person of reasonable intelligence can achieve much more than a gifted person, provided he or she wants to do so. This is true of other spheres also. For instance, in the world of sports, once a certain level of skill and ability is present, it is the will to excel that counts above all. Everyone admires the seemingly effortless grace and fluidity of the Brazilian soccer team, but it is easy to forget the will to win that is behind the sublime display of skill, a will so tenacious that it involves years of hard work before the spotlight ever shines on any of these players.

It is not the brightest people who are necessarily the best at study. It is the people who want to be best, and who methodically and patiently dedicate themselves to the task of study. They are more likely to achieve something than the wayward and haphazard genius. It is reassuring to know that you do not need to be of Einstein's caliber to make a success of study. What is vital is what *you want*. If you really want to study well, you will find a way to realise your desire.

The great Greek philosopher Aristotle begins his *Metaphysics* with the famous assertion, 'all human beings by nature desire to know'. So study is not alien to our nature. The famous Jesuit thinker Bernard Lonergan, who taught at the Pontifical Gregorian University in Rome, talked of 'the pure unrestricted desire to know'. We have inside of us, according to Lonergan and others, the desire for unconditional and perfect truth. Saint Augustine put it in a more appealing way at the beginning of his *Confessions*, 'For thou hast made us for thyself and our hearts are restless until they rest in Thee.' John Henry Cardinal Newman, author of *The idea of a university* and founding rector of the Catholic University of Ireland, now University College Dublin, where Cardinal Connell was professor of general metaphysics for many years, described in glowing terms the desire animating the university professor: 'It [the university] is the place where the professor becomes eloquent, and is a missionary and a preacher, displaying his science in its most complete and most winning form, pouring it forth with the zeal of enthusiasm, and lighting up his own love of it in the breasts of his students.'

Jesus values the will, he takes our desires seriously. In fact, the first words ever attributed to Jesus in the gospel of John are words that question the nature and intensity of our desires. Recall that even before Jesus himself speaks in the gospel of John, the prologue has begun by describing him as the *logos* (Jn 1:1), this Greek word with a generous range of meaning, which evokes warm intelligence and rich rationality – the creative word, the thought full of meaning, the wisdom of God. The *logos* expresses God perfectly and reveals God to man. Jesus' opening question will express God perfectly and reveal something God-like to the first disciples.

When two disciples start to follow Jesus in John 1:37, he asks a 'question' – our English word comes from the Latin verb *quaerere*, meaning 'to seek'. Jesus sees them following him and asks, 'What do you desire?' (Jn 1:38). This is an enormous question. Jesus is not simply asking them what they intend to do at that moment, or what they want to eat later on. Certainly he is asking them a question that is formulated in the present tense, yet it relates to their future. It relates not simply to a particular moment in their future, but to their whole future, the whole story of their

lives. He is asking them what kind of people they want to become. This is a
profound question. It goes to the depths. Jesus is not asking them how
much money they want to make, how famous they want to become, how
secure they want their careers to be. He is not talking about the kinds of
desires that our society helps manufacture, or that our egoism pushes us
towards.

Jesus is not referring to the desires that are produced by these two disciples or by their culture. He is honing in on the desires that they *discover*
within themselves, not on the desires they themselves create. These deepest
desires are rooted in God, the source of desire. And because they are
grounded in God, they are infinite desires. Note that Jesus does not ask
them to express desires that can be realised within a definite time-frame, or
to limit themselves to feasible and viable desires.

TRUTH

Deep down, each of us discovers a primordial desire for truth, a desire we
ourselves have not implanted. In the spirituality of study, the desire for
truth is central. Children, who are still innocent, ceaselessly express it.
They persistently ask the question, 'Why?' You give them an answer, but
this only elicits another question. And it goes on and on until you say
something like, 'Well, it's just because, and that's enough questions for
now.' Children, without realising it, are looking for total truth, complete
intelligibility, and so they will not refrain from questions as long as a full
and comprehensive answer to everything continues to elude them. Of
course, the questions of children express more than the desire for truth.
They are also a plea for a listening ear from parents, a call for reassurance
from adults, a quest for stability in the midst of world that changes continually before their eyes.

This desire for truth is central to a spirituality of study. This is the
desire to uncover what is deepest in things. It is the desire to find out what
they are. Some students and scholars get distracted by what is interesting,
and so they neglect what is true. Just as someone can become infatuated

with physical beauty, so too the mind can be seduced by flamboyant and witty ideas, by complex notions that hide an essential emptiness.

Postmodern thought, now in decline, is an extreme example of this self-indulgent sophistry. Postmodern thinkers delight in cultivating an obscure style that defies comprehension. They play with a thousand possibilities and defer as much as they can any contact with reality. They seek to appear profound while skating capriciously on the surface. They wrongly presume that complexity equals depth. It is certainly true that issues are not always straightforward. But when thinkers needlessly complicate things, their complexity does not spell depth, but death, the death of the possibility of encountering truth. Although postmodernism no longer enjoys the preeminence it did a decade ago, it still affects our way of thinking. There is a tendency for individuals to presume they possess their own individual truth, one they have found for themselves and that 'feels' right, there is a tendency to believe that things are true because individuals decide they are true. There is widespread skepticism about the possibility of arriving at communal or ultimate truth. Therefore the intellectual quest of seeking the truth seems useless and purposeless.

Postmodernism is a kind of relativism. Unfortunately, many prospective students in western society suffer from a distinctly relativist handicap when it comes to searching for the truth. If Allan Bloom's grim diagnosis is to be believed, practically every student arrives at university with the conviction that truth is relative.[3] Although Bloom is guilty of exaggeration, he nevertheless highlights a widespread and dysfunctional stance toward truth in western culture. There are various reasons for it, among which are intellectual laziness, self-deception, the egoism of thinking that ultimately only oneself exists, a refusal to accept that the truth of things can and should limit what one ought to do, a fear of being anything other than

3   'There is one thing a professor can be absolutely certain of: almost every student entering the university believes, or says he believes, that truth is relative. If this belief is put to the test, one can count on the students' reaction: they will be uncomprehending. That anyone should regard the proposition as not self-evident astonishes them, as though he were calling into question 2 + 2 = 4': A. Bloom, *The closing of the American mind* (New York, 1987), p. 25.

terminally nice and politically correct. Truth is preferably made to order, custom-designed to fit each person's particular needs. Relativism is so deeply engrained in western culture that many westerners are blind to its destructiveness, and are ironically proud of it as a sign of cultural sophistication. Its lethal effect is not always initially evident: indeed, at first glance it seems rather benign to encourage everyone to do their own thing. The problem is that the 'thing' in question that they have been mandated to do can turn out to be anything but innocuous.

Fundamentalism is another enemy of truth. It presumes that we are already in possession of the truth even before we begin to search for it. And so it declares that the quest for truth is unnecessary because its adherents already have it. It relieves people of the obligation and right to think for themselves. Fundamentalism thrives in the absence of solid education. If people are not urged to learn, if there is little social support for the development of reasoning powers, if right and rigorous thinking is discouraged, then fundamentalism can easily become a dominant social force.

The purpose of study is to seek the truth. Postmodernist and fundamentalist ways of thinking are hostile to truth in different ways. Postmodernism and relativism claim that we can never arrive at ultimate truth. Fundamentalism pretends that we are already in possession of ultimate truth.

LIBERATING TRUTH

The reason why a Christian seeks the truth is in order to share it with others, in order to light up their lives. The impact of truth is extraordinary. It promotes the trust that is vital for the continuing existence of society. After all, it if we do not believe in the honesty or reliability of our fellow citizens, there is no point in cooperating with them, since they may not honor their commitment. We end up losing all respect for each other, since nobody can be counted on to tell things as they are.

Jesus was called master because he taught and educated people the truth. His teaching was a work of mercy (instructing the ignorant) to the minds and souls of those around him. The poverty of individuals who lack the truth is not physically evident like material poverty. But its effects are devastating, leading to intellectual and moral bankruptcy. If individuals do not know the difference between right and wrong, if they have a mistaken notion of the goal of life, if they do not know what goodness is or how to become good, they are leading incredibly deprived lives. The truth that frees people is the truth that is not simply recognised intellectually, but also and above all *lived*. When we put truth into practice, it makes us free.

'The truth shall make you free' (Jn 8:32) is one of the better-known sayings of Jesus. But it is a lesser-known fact that this phrase is embedded in a longer statement, where Jesus says that keeping his teaching and putting it into practice demonstrates that we are his disciples, and this enables us to know the truth, the truth that will set us free. We cannot arrive at this liberating truth in the world of study unless we live in an upright way. We are invited to combine orthodoxy with orthopraxis, true knowledge with right action. There is a fundamental unity in our lives, and therefore knowing and doing should form a unity. We need to put the truth into practice.

We cannot live justly outside of the context of relationships: we must acknowledge our dependence upon God, as well as learning from outstanding minds and the great books. We can also learn an enormous amount from peers and colleagues, from discussing and exchanging ideas with friends who are also animated by the love of truth. That is why it is dangerous to confuse freedom with complete autonomy. Certain people imagine that the ties of faith and the claims of tradition and authority are actually shackles. In fact, these bonds are really anchors that give us solidity in the sea of life, and roots that help us flourish and grow. Without these fruitful and stabilising links, we are left without points of reference, without models to look up to, without a direction to take.

STUDIOUSNESS

In Chapter 2 of his book *The intellectual life*, A.G. Sertillanges discusses the virtue proper to the intellectual. This virtue is studiousness. At first glance, it seems more than obvious that studiousness is the virtue proper to the intellectual. However, the virtue of studiousness is not as straightforward or as easily comprehensible as we may initially presume.

Sertillanges points out that Thomas Aquinas places studiousness under the virtue of temperance. In other words, we have to moderate or temper studiousness. This is because there are two excesses in knowledge, one in each direction, and each of these excesses is a vice. One excess or vice is negligence, not caring about study, not bothering about it, neglecting it, being slapdash and slipshod about study. The vice of negligence is fairly obvious, and we don't need to say a lot about it.

The other excess or vice is curiosity. This is often a more subtle vice, a fault that is more difficult to detect. Curiosity means that someone thirsts so much for knowledge, wants knowledge so much, that he or she begins to subordinate everything else to it. All else is discarded or relegated to a secondary position – prayer, duties to one's family, obligations to one's religious community, and so on. But if our thirst for knowledge becomes so intense that we forget our duties as human beings, then we will end up being less than human, and inhumane. Curiosity can also mean that someone goes off on a completely different tangent in study, not what they are supposed to investigate, but something fundamentally dissimilar. Of course, it is good to have a healthy range of interests, but if someone's task is to study theology, it makes sense to keep away from astrophysics!

Another way in which curiosity manifests itself is when someone stretches beyond what they can truly reach, when they are overly ambitious. Sertillanges quotes a striking phrase from Thomas Aquinas: 'I want you to decide to go to the sea by the streams, not directly.' Don't jump in the deep end, in other words! In the words of Sertillanges: 'Don't overload the foundation, do not carry the building higher than the base permits, or before it has been made secure: otherwise the whole structure would collapse.'[4] So don't overestimate your powers or your capacities.

The ability to judge ourselves truly and wisely is worth a lot. As Sertillanges puts it: 'You have a part that only you can play; and your busi-

4   A.G. Sertillanges, *The intellectual life*, p. 28.

ness is to play it to perfection, instead of trying to force fortune. Our lives are not interchangeable. Equally by aiming too high and by falling too low, one misses the path to the goal. Go straight ahead, in your own way, with God for guide.'[5]

SUMMING UP

I have stressed the importance of a spirituality of study, the cultural obstacles to it, its centrality as a Christian commandment, the crucial role of desire and the desire for truth, the dangers of postmodernism, relativism, and fundamentalism, the liberating truth of a knowledge that harmonizes with our way of life, and finally the importance of the virtue of studiousness.

Perhaps a useful way of finishing this article is with some questions that invite us to reflect on the place of study in our lives. What works for me best when it comes to study? What does not? What are my strengths in the area of study? What are my weaknesses? What direction am I going in? What direction should I be going in? Looking beyond this particular paper, next week's test, my college degree, etc., what are my goals in study? What is the purpose and desire that drives it? What is the universal good for which I am studying? How can I nourish my vision? How can I expand my imagination? Can I visualise where I want study to take me? Who are the people I am studying for? How can study help them? How can I better communicate the results of my study to them? As part of the community of the church, how can I better share my talents with those of others? How can I practically cooperate in study with others? How can I strengthen the sense of being called to study? How can I reinforce my belief in the importance of the intellectual life? Can I believe more and more that God's love for me is being articulated through the invitation to develop my intellect?

5   Ibid., p. 29.

Titian, *Noli me tangere*

Noli me tangere! Painting sacramental life

LIAM BERGIN

TITIAN (TIZIANO VECELLIO) WAS THE GREATEST painter of sixteenth-century Venice, the first to achieve European fame in his lifetime.[1] Born at Pieve di Cadore in the Veneto around 1490, he had a long and prolific career until his death in 1576. His *Noli me tangere*, hanging in the National Gallery in London since 1856, was painted while the artist was still in his twenties. The painting represents the meeting between the Risen Christ and Mary of Magdala as recounted in John 20:1–18.

The gospel of John locates the meeting between Jesus and Mary Magdalene in a garden near the tomb of Jesus. Titian opts for a broader setting with a Venetian hamlet on the right and with the landscape dissolving into a watery haze on the left. The encounter is with the crucified and risen Lord. The passion is clearly recalled by the nail mark that is seen on Jesus' right foot. Through the power of the resurrection, the bruised body has been raised to life and the burial shroud has been cast off in favour of a white garment that is bathed in splendid light. Like many of the works of his Venetian predecessors, Titian's painting is radiant with light and colour: white, blue, red and green immediately impact the eyes of the viewer.

At the centre of the painting there is a tree which divides the canvas in two. Rising diagonally to fill the top left corner, it delineates two worlds, one sacred, one profane. To the left of the tree Christ is represented in his risen state. Clouds in the top left of the canvas barely conceal the morning sun and the fullness of light and life which the ascended Lord will soon enjoy in the eternal presence of the Father. To the right, Mary of Magdala kneels and stretches out to touch the figure that she had mistakenly identified with the gardener. Above her, a blue sky hangs over a typical

1 See C. Hope, 'Titian's life and times' in *Titian* (London, 2003), pp 9–28.

sixteenth-century Venetian *borgo* where normal life unfolds. Looking closely, we can even see a man walking his dog!

The tree defines the respective spaces occupied by Jesus and Mary. Yet, there are two points of penetration. The hand of Jesus extends to the right; the tentative, seeking hand of Mary that extends from the left, offers a balance. The tree ensures that the traditional theological distinction between the spheres of nature and grace is maintained. Nevertheless, the extended hands remind the viewers that the risen Lord breaches time and space and enters our world and, in response, invites us to seek him out. The timber of the tree rising behind Christ reminds us of the wood of the cross. But the former instrument of death now bears leaves and branches and is transformed into a life-giving membrane between heaven and earth, separating and uniting both orders at once.

Compositionally, this painting is built on triangles.[2] There is an outer triangle from the top of the tree to the base of the picture, enclosing much of the natural scene and the two main figures. A second, inner triangle is formed by the figures themselves, extending downwards from the head of Christ and closed by the line from his right foot across to the robe of Mary Magdalene. The outer triangle delineates the order of creation; the inner one marks the order of redemption. Theologically the point is clear: by becoming human, the Son of God embraces all of creation and the fallen world is saved from within. But there is a third triangle, inside the second, right at the heart of the painting.

The out-stretched arms close this space at the centre of the painting. It is framed on the left by the torso of Jesus, on the top and right by his outstretched hand and the handle of the hoe and it is closed on the bottom by the line from Mary's head and shoulders to her outstretched hand and arm. This space may well be taken to signify the church, the heart of the encounter between the risen Lord and humankind. There is little to be seen in this space: to the right, close to the Magdalene, is the terrain of the garden; the left, close to Jesus, is obscured by the white cloak that hangs

2   The author is grateful to the artist Carmel Mooney for her comments on the composition of this painting. He also acknowledges the historical insights provided by Dr Eileen Kane.

from his shoulder. The space is delineated by earth and heaven, human and divine, sinner and saviour. It is penetrated by dark and light, suffering and joy, absence and presence. It is shaped by man and woman, bridegroom and bride, lover and beloved. It is bounded by restlessness and peace, yearning and fulfilment, longing and desire. The eye of the viewer is always drawn back to this ecclesial place at the heart of the painting, to the centre of the triangle formed by the counterpoised bodies of Jesus and Mary. On this the painting stands or falls. The right hand side, we have noted, is formed by the hoe and the head and shoulder of the Magdalene. If this central space can be interpreted ecclesiologically, the hoe must find a sacramental hermeneutic. The hoe is the standard of the risen Christ, the sign and instrument of his victory. It traverses the interface created by the tree-cross. It is the hoe that brings Christ's hand from left to right, from the sacred sphere to the profane, while crossing through the central ecclesial space. Saint Thomas and the scholastics spoke of the sacraments using the concept of instrumental causality, but here there is more.

FROM A TROUBLED PLACE

First of all, there is disbelief and misunderstanding. The Gospel of John tells us that Mary is in the garden, close by the tomb, weeping. To the right of the painting Titian has replaced Jerusalem with a nameless *borgo* that could have been anywhere in his native sixteenth-century Veneto. Ancient mosaics in the basilicas of Rome and beyond often depict the two towns of Bethlehem and Jerusalem on either side of the triumphal arch that frames the entrance to the sanctuary. These arches normally have the *chi-rho* monogram of the Christ or some other christological symbol at the top of the arch. The span represents the saving extent of Jesus' life from womb to tomb and the redemption that is consequently communicated to all who participate in this mystery through the liturgy whoever they may be and wherever they may come from. Biblical scholars are unable to identify where Luke's village of Emmaus is to be found today. Ironically, however, because Emmaus is nowhere in particular it can be everywhere. Titian makes a similar point in placing the nameless *borgo* as part of the backdrop for this encounter. It can be everywhere that women and men struggle with the concrete circumstances of their lives and try to find some meaning within them. It can be every place where hopes and expectations are dashed as unforeseen events rupture former certainties and convictions.

The dialogue between Mary and the angels shows that she knows something of what has happened because she has seen the empty tomb. But she but does not understand. The angels ask, 'Woman, why are you weeping?' Mary replies 'They have taken my Lord away and I don't know where they have put him.' Then she turns around and meets the stranger whom she presumes to be the gardener. Indeed, X-ray analysis of Titian's painting shows that Christ was originally depicted wearing a gardener's hat and turning away from the Magdalene. Initially, their dialogue does not resolve anything. Jesus repeats the question posed by the angels: 'Woman, why are you weeping?' Mary's response reveals that she is still with the dead Christ: 'Sir, if you have taken him away, tell me where you have put him, and I will go and remove him.' Everything is at a standstill in Mary's mind: she is still shut up in the tomb of death with Jesus, and her difficulties are as heavy as the stone that closed the entrance. Surely this encounter between Mary and the gardener is going nowhere. But maybe something deeper is about to be revealed!

DECIPHERED BY THE WORD

Through a dialogue informed by the scriptures there is a moment of awakening. It is only when Jesus speaks Mary's name that she recognises him. Jesus and Mary had met before. All four gospels refer to Mary of Magdala as one of the female disciples who followed Jesus and witnessed the events at Golgotha. In the gospels of Matthew, Mark and John, Mary's presence as a witness to the crucifixion is mentioned (Mt 27:56; 27:61; Mk 15:40; 15:47; 16:1; Jn 19:25). In the gospel of Luke 8:2, Mary is recorded as the woman 'from whom seven demons had gone out'. More significantly, however, Mary of Magdala is listed by all four evangelists as one of the first witnesses to the resurrection (Mt 28:1; Mk 16:9; Lk 24:10; Jn 20:1–18). Contemporary biblical scholarship acknowledges that Mary of Magdala or Mary Magdalene is not the same person as Mary of Bethany, the sister of Lazarus and Martha, the one who witnessed her brother's restoration to life (Jn 11:1), who anointed the feet of Jesus (Jn 12:3) and who had chosen 'the better part' while her sister Martha was 'preoccupied with so many things' (Lk 10:38–42). Nor is Mary Magdalene to be confused with the woman accused of adultery (Jn 8:1–11). Nevertheless, such confusion did take place over the centuries, probably due to the close proximity in Luke's gospel of the accounts of the 'woman who had a bad name' who anoints the feet of Jesus (Lk 7:36–8) and the inclusion among Jesus' disciples of 'Mary surnamed the Magdalene, from whom seven demons had gone out' (Lk 8:2). As Raymond E. Brown remarks,

> In the popular mind, under the influence of the Lucan picture of a sinful woman, the woman of Bethany (Mary, according to John) was soon characterised as a sinner. Then, for good measure, this sinful Mary of Bethany was identified with Mary of Magdala from whom seven devils had been cast out (Luke 7:2) and who went to the tomb of Jesus. And so, for instance, the Catholic liturgy came to honour in a single feast all three women (the sinner of Galilee, Mary of Bethany, Mary of Magdala) as one saint – a confusion that has existed in the western Church, although not without a demure, since the time of Gregory the Great.[3]

In fact, this mistaken identification is to be found in Titian's painting and in much of the traditional iconography that surrounds Mary Magdalene in art. Here, as elsewhere, Mary of Magdala is represented with a jar, a clear allusion to the oil used to anoint the feet of Jesus by the Johannine Mary of Bethany and by the Lucan 'woman who had a bad name'.

Consequently, the relationship between Jesus and Mary as represented by Titian is even more significant than that allowed by a historical-critical

3   R.L. Brown, *The gospel according to John*, I (London, 1966), p. 452.

reading of the biblical texts. When Jesus comes to raise Lazarus he is moved by the sight of Mary's tears and asks her, 'Where have you put him?' These words are echoed by the Magdalene as she grieves by the tomb and tells the angels, 'I don't know where they have put him.' Then, in the raising of Lazarus from the dead, Mary comes to know Jesus as the one over whom death does not hold the final word. Six days before the Passover, Mary of Bethany had anointed the feet of Jesus and lovingly wiped them with her hair. This extravagant gesture that scandalised the onlookers had heralded Jesus' death and burial. Together, these actions (recounted in consecutive chapters in John's gospel) announce Jesus' imminent death and his impending resurrection. As the Magdalene searches for the missing Lord in the garden by the tomb, ironically she carries the clue to his whereabouts in her hand. In speaking Mary's name, Jesus recalls the power of these previous encounters and opens to her the meaning of the scriptures that he should die and rise again. Only then does Mary come to faith, a faith that will need to be affirmed not only by word but also by action.

INFORMED BY A SACRAMENTAL ACTION

The oldest baptismal texts suggest that from earliest times the rites of Christian initiation were celebrated as part of the Easter vigil. The encounter between Jesus and Mary takes place 'very early on the first day of the week and still dark' (Jn 20:1). Immediately there is a vigil-like atmosphere and the liturgical context is set. Mary recognises Jesus when he speaks her name. At the heart of baptism is the naming of the catechumen. It is the moment when the candidate is informed of his or her dignity as a son or daughter of God. When this word is spoken in the church it is the voice of the risen Lord that is heard. But the word of grace that is proclaimed is also informed by a sacramental gesture.

The disciples on the road to Emmaus recognise Jesus in the breaking of the bread. Luke takes care in describing the actions at table: 'he took bread, blessed and broke it, and gave it to them' (Lk 24:30). In this verbal structure the evangelist is deliberately alluding to the church's celebration of the eucharist. Other elements of the story reinforce this interpretation: the encounter takes place on the first day of the week, the day of the Christian gathering; the scriptures interpret the experience of the disciples just as they shape the faith of the Christian assembly; and, the encounter with Christ takes place in the ritual, the sacramental action of the church. A similar structure is to be found in Titian's representation of this post-Easter encounter.

Titian places a jar in the foreground of the painting in Mary's left hand. Stretching out her right arm as she seeks to grasp the risen Lord, her left hand holds the perfumed nard that had prophetically foretold his fate. In this moment of recognition, the ritual anointing is brought to the fore. Titian frames this drama between water and oil, neither of which is mentioned in the Johannine account. Surely this inclusion is a reference to baptism, the washing with water and the anointing with oil that is at once a dying with Christ so as to rise to new life with him? The synoptic gospels recount that the Roman soldiers who crucified Jesus and witnessed his death came to believe in him 'as a son of God' (Mk 15:39; Mt 27:54) or as 'a great man' (Lk 23:47). No such confession is found in the fourth gospel. But, when the soldiers pierce Jesus' side with a lance, 'there came out blood and water' (Jn 19:34), symbols of eucharist and baptism. In the Johannine scheme, faith in the risen Christ is mediated not through witnessing his death on the cross but in an ecclesial encounter with the scriptural word informed by a sacramental gesture.

The post-conciliar revision of the rites of the Catholic church places the liturgy of the word as an indispensable, prior moment in the ritual celebration of each sacrament. But the progression from word to sacrament is not merely a matter of sequence. The sacraments communicate the saving mystery proclaimed in the word in a new and radical way. While both word and sacrament express and communicate the salvific power of God, there is an inherent intensity and deepening of the divine revelation and self-communication in the church as we move from ambo to altar.

MEDIATED BY ABSENCE

Mary does not touch or hold Jesus. As soon as he reveals himself to her she reaches out in love: 'Rabbuni!, Master!', she confesses. Jesus responds '*Noli me tangere* – do not cling to me.' The passage from non-faith to faith requires that we abandon the desire to cling, to touch, to hold. Faith begins with a renunciation of the immediate and with an assent to the mediation of the church. From now on, it is impossible to touch his physical body; we can encounter him only as mediated through the church. We hear him in the scriptures re-read as his own words; we meet him in the sacraments performed as his own gestures; we see him in the ethical witness of women and men who incarnate his own service. These are the realities to which we cling while we await in hope the return of the Lord. In this final revelation we shall see God face to face as we share forever the fullness of divine life.

MISSIONED BY VISION

Mary's response to the encounter is to go and tell the disciples that 'she had seen the Lord and that he had said these things to her' (Jn 20:18). Like the disciples on the road to Emmaus, there is a compulsion to return to Jerusalem to witness to the risen Lord. Their immediate reaction is to participate in the church's mission to 'go and tell'. In the fourth gospel, the call to mission and the ethics of service are carefully accented. In John, the synoptic account of the institution of the eucharist is intentionally substituted by the washing of the feet. The order to repeat the ritual actions – 'do this in memory of me' – is replaced by the ethical command 'I have given you an example so that you may copy what I have done to you' (Jn 13:15). In this way *leitourgia* and *diakonia/marturia* are intrinsically linked. Service is not a corollary or a secondary moment to liturgy but is constitutive of the sacramental encounter. Christian ethics do not have a derived moral value but are demanded as a theological testimony to the truth of Jesus' resurrection. That is why, in his apostolic letter for the year of the eucharist, *Mane nobiscum Domine*, Pope John Paul II reminds us that 'The Eucharist is not merely an expression of communion in the Church's life; it is also a *project of solidarity* for all of humanity.'[4] This point is reiterated by Pope Benedict XVI in his encyclical letter *Deus caritas est*:

> The church's deepest nature is expressed in her three-fold responsibility: of proclaiming the word of God (*kerygma-martyria*), celebrating the sacraments (*leitourgia*), and exercising the ministry of charity (*diakonia*). These duties presuppose each other and are inseparable. For the Church, charity is not a kind of welfare activity which could equally well be left to others, but is a part of her nature, an indispensable expression of her very being.[5]

RETURNING HOME

In the middle ground of Titian's painting we see a flock of sheep already journeying towards the heavenly pastures, yet clouds veil the fullness of divine presence. The white cloak around Mary's shoulders reflects the light of Christ, yet the red gown ties her to the earth. Her gaze passes through the central space and is fixed on the Lord. Our attention is drawn once more to the significance of the ecclesial space at the heart of Titian's painting in which this divine-human drama is revealed. This drama unfolds in the liturgy of the church.

When the ecclesial community celebrates a sacrament, it unveils in the present the power of the future. *Sacrosanctum concilium*, Vatican II's constitution on the liturgy, insists on the eschatological dimension of the rites of the church. Every liturgy, it states, is a foretaste of the liturgy of the heavenly Jerusalem. It is interesting that this eschatological aspect of the liturgy is the leitmotif of *Spiritus et sponsa*, the apostolic letter of Pope John Paul II on the fortieth anniversary of the council document. 'What, indeed, is the liturgy other than the voice of the Holy Spirit and the Bride, holy Church,

4   John Paul II, *Mane nobiscum Domine*, 27.
5   Benedict XVI, *Deus caritas est*, 25.

crying in unison to the Lord Jesus: "Come"? What is the liturgy other than that pure, inexhaustible source of "living water" from which all who thirst can freely draw the gift of God?'[6] Approaching the sacraments from an eschatological perspective brings the church face to face with its future. Salvation has been won in Jesus Christ but awaits fulfilment in the history of each believer. Such an approach also opens the church and its members to the unknown that inevitably lurks in the tension between inauguration and fulfilment.

Titian's Christ gazes at Mary but his feet are facing us. Inherently there is an invitation addressed to every viewer. It is a call to faith. It is a challenge to enter into the ecclesial space opened up by the encounter between Christ and Mary. Like Mary, we too often inhabit a troubled place; we too reach out hoping to touch the divine; we too want to cling to the risen Lord. But like the Magdalene we are drawn to a space where the word deciphers our experience, the sacramental action anticipates our destiny and the call to service reveals our identity as children of God. With Mary we are called by name; we are clothed in the white garment of rebirth; we are anointed with the oil of salvation. '*Noli me tangere* – do not cling.' Titian reminds us to 'go and tell' the Good News until we come to that new space that is a new heaven and a new earth (Rev 21:1), where we see God face to face (1 Cor 13:12), and where God is all in all (1 Cor 15:28). It is a space where *Noli me tangere* is no more.

---

6   John Paul II, *Spiritus et Sponsa*, 1.

'Ministers of your joy': Pope Benedict XVI on the priesthood

JOSEPH MURPHY

ADDRESSING HIS FELLOW CARDINALS on the day before his election to the chair of Peter, the then Cardinal Joseph Ratzinger spoke of the pastoral ministry, recalling Christ's command to the apostles to bear fruit that will last (John 15:16). Explaining that the fruit in question is all that has been sown in human hearts: 'love, knowledge, a gesture capable of touching hearts, words that open the soul to joy in the Lord', he prayed on that occasion that the Lord would 'once again give us a shepherd according to his own heart, a shepherd who will guide us to knowledge of Christ, to his love and to true joy'.[1] At the beginning of his pontificate, Pope Benedict XVI returned to this theme, describing the shepherd's task as one of imitating Christ's mission of seeking out the sheep that have strayed into the desert to lead them 'towards the place of life, towards friendship with the Son of God, towards the One who gives us life, and life in abundance'. To feed the sheep means to love them and to be ready to suffer for and on account of them. Loving means 'giving the sheep what is truly good, the nourishment of God's truth, of God's Word, the nourishment of his presence, which he gives us in the blessed sacrament'. The purpose of the priest's life, the pope said, is 'to reveal God to men' and the pastoral ministry is ultimately 'a service to joy, to God's joy which longs to break into the world'.[2]

Throughout the first year of his pontificate, this vision of the shepherd's task, which draws on the words of the gospel and the writings of the

1 J. Ratzinger, Homily at the Mass for the Election of the Roman Pontiff, *L'Osservatore Romano*, 20 April 2005 (English translation slightly modified).
2 Benedict XVI, Homily at the Mass for the Inauguration of the Pontificate, *L'Osservatore Romano*, 27 April 2005.

church fathers, has been very much to the fore in the Holy Father's teaching on priestly life and ministry. In the course of the year, the pope held three meetings with groups of priests and deacons: two with the clergy of the diocese of Rome and one with the clergy of Aosta. Apart from these encounters, which took the form of highly instructive and insightful question-and-answer sessions on priestly ministry and spirituality, and on the practical pastoral problems which priests daily encounter, Pope Benedict had occasion to speak about the priesthood at the ordination ceremony in Saint Peter's basilica on Pentecost Sunday (15 May 2005), at his meeting with seminarians during his visit to Cologne in August 2005 for the World Youth Day celebrations and at the Chrism Mass on Holy Thursday 2006. His stirring words on all these occasions evinced a lifetime's theological reflection on the nature of the priesthood, a reflection which became particularly intense in the years following the Second Vatican Council, due to the doubts raised at the time about the essence and purpose of the priesthood.[3]

3   Some of Joseph Ratzinger's more significant contributions to the theology of priesthood and priestly spirituality are: 'Zur Frage nach dem Sinn des priesterlichen Dienstes' in *Geist und Liebe* 41 (1968), 347–76; 'Il ministero sacerdotale' in *L'Osservatore Romano*, 28 May 1970; 'The priest as mediator and minister of Christ in the light of the message of the new testament' in *Principles of Catholic theology* (San Francisco, 1987), pp 267–84; *Ministers of your joy: reflections on priestly spirituality* (Slough, 1988); 'The male priesthood: a violation of women's rights?' in Congregation for the Doctrine of the Faith, *From 'Inter insigniores' to 'Ordinatio sacerdotalis': documents and commentaries* (Vatican City, 1996), pp 142–50; 'On the essence of the priesthood' in *Called to communion: understanding the church today* (San Francisco, 1996), pp 105–31; 'Preparation for priestly ministry' in *A new song for the Lord* (New York, 1996), pp 206–26; 'The ministry and life of priests' in *Pilgrim fellowship of faith: the church as communion* (San Francisco, 2005), pp 153–75. 'The priest as mediator and minister' is the revised form of a lecture first given at the Maynooth Union summer school in 1969; the various papers, including Ratzinger's, are published in G. Meagher (ed.), *Priest: person and ministry* (Dublin and London, 1970).

DEBATE ON THE NATURE OF THE PRIESTHOOD

According to the traditional christocentric, ontological and sacramental understanding, the priesthood is rooted in the being of the man who ministers. It is conferred by Christ through the mediation of the church in the sacrament of holy orders in such a way that the priest is conformed to him in order to act *in persona Christi*, and it is centred on the celebration of the eucharistic sacrifice and the other sacraments. Although preaching and guidance of the community were seen as typically priestly activities, there was a tendency among some authors, drawing on the description of Christ's priesthood in the Letter to the Hebrews, to locate the essence of the priesthood exclusively in its cultic dimension and to see the other aspects as subordinate to the celebration of the sacraments.

In the 1960s, a more social and functional view came to the fore, which describes the priesthood in terms of a ministry to the congregation within the social institution called the church.[4] This view places greater emphasis on the priest's role as leader of the community and preacher of the Word, but, in its more extreme forms, it can result in the practical exclusion of the cultic aspects. Sometimes, where the essential distinction between the sacramentally ordained priesthood and the common baptismal priesthood of all the faithful becomes blurred, the priesthood comes to be interpreted in sociological rather than sacramental terms. The priest is then seen merely as an administrator and preacher, a representative of the church or the local community, rather than of Christ. As a consequence, some hold that it is possible to delegate a lay member of the faithful to carry out priestly functions where the sacramental needs of the local community require it.[5]

---

4   On the various approaches to the theology of the priesthood in the postconciliar period, see E. Castellucci, *Il ministero sacerdotale* (Brescia, 2002), pp 248–62.

5   E. Schillebeeckx, who understands ministry primarily in terms of 'leadership of the community,' may be cited as an example; see his *Ministry: a case for change* (London, 1981); idem, *The church with a human face: a new and expanded theology of ministry* (London, 1985). The Congregation for the Doctrine of the Faith responded to the reductive functionalist understanding of the priesthood of the type promoted by Schillebeeckx, among others, in its 1983 letter *Sacerdotium ministeriale*.

Variants of this functional model of the priesthood arose for diverse reasons, including the cultural upheavals of the time, a tendency to view the church and, consequently, the priesthood in purely sociological terms, a new-found interest in the ideas of the sixteenth-century reformers and the influence of radical exegetical theories which tended to read scripture in separation from the church's tradition and to over-emphasise the discontinuity between the old testament and the new.[6]

Symptomatic of the new sociological and functional approach is the report on ministry prepared for the Dutch pastoral council which took place at Noordwijkerhout in 1970, according to which 'the ministry consists of the mission and the power, officially conferred by the christian community, of presiding over the community in accordance with the gospel by introducing it to the meaning of life and supplying the inspiration for all its activities in this world'.[7] Nowhere in the report was reference made to the institution by Christ of the priesthood or indeed of the church herself. Ministry was interpreted in purely sociological terms as an office of leadership in the church, the precise form of which could be changed to reflect the evolving needs of the community. This conception was taken to task by the assembly to which it was presented, and the definition was amended by adding that the minister is 'a witness, commissioned and accountable, of the definitive deed of salvation in Jesus Christ'. Although this definition was an improvement, it remained insufficient and still smacked too much of an exclusively functional and community-based notion of the ministry.[8]

In its different forms, this new conception, because of the doubts it raised about the nature and purpose of the priestly ministry, provoked a deep and long-lasting identity crisis among priests, which led to many departures from the priesthood and a dramatic decline in vocations. At the 1971 synod of bishops, the participants were acutely aware of the spiritual

6   For a brief account, see T.J. McGovern, *Priestly identity: a study in the theology of priesthood* (Dublin, 2002), pp 7–13.
7   Quoted in J. Galot, *Theology of the priesthood*, trans. R. Balducelli (San Francisco, 1985), p. 17 (translation slightly modified).
8   Ibid., p. 18.

crisis which they blamed on a defective theological understanding of the very nature of the priesthood.[9] It was clear from the synod discussions that fresh commitment to the priestly vocation could only come about if the theological underpinnings of the priesthood itself were clearly understood. To this end, in its final document *De sacerdotio ministeriali*, the synod laid down the relevant doctrinal principles and provided a series of practical orientations for priestly life and ministry.

Pope John Paul II made his own contribution to the theology of the priesthood in his annual Holy Thursday letters to priests and in the series of eighteen general audience catecheses dedicated to the priesthood between March and September 1993. In addition, the work of the 1971 synod of bishops was complemented by that of the synod held in 1990, which was concerned with priestly formation and resulted in Pope John Paul's post-synodal apostolic exhortation *Pastores dabo vobis*, published in 1992. This document, which contains a succinct theological account of the nature and mission of the ministerial priesthood in its second chapter, provides the blueprint for the training of priests today.

The various interventions of the papal magisterium since the Second Vatican Council developed and clarified the conciliar teaching on the priesthood, which is found above all in the Dogmatic Constitution on the Church *Lumen gentium* (*LG*) and the Decree on the Life and Ministry of Priests *Presbyterorum ordinis* (*PO*). The council fathers, aware that the traditional conception of the priesthood in cultic and sacrificial terms was somewhat restrictive, sought to present that understanding within a more complete description of the nature of the ordained ministry in its different grades. Reflecting the discussion on the episcopate, which led to the formulation of *Lumen gentium*, 18–27, the council, especially in *Lumen gentium*, 28 and *Presbyterorum ordinis*, 2, traced a portrait of the priest in ministerial and missionary terms. The priesthood is seen as deriving from the mission of Christ and inserted within the mission of the church as a whole. In *Lumen gentium*, 28 and *Presbyterorum ordinis*, 4–6 the content of

9   Cf. Synod of Bishops, *De sacerdotio ministeriali* in *Acta Apostolicae Sedis* 68 (1971) 898–922.

the priest's mission was expressed by reference to his sharing in the three *munera* of Christ: prophet, priest and king. Accordingly, the priest, in a manner subordinate to the bishop, is ordained to preach, celebrate the sacraments and provide pastoral leadership for the faithful. These are not three separate tasks but three aspects of the same ministry, so much so that to speak of one is to speak implicitly of the other two. Preaching is directed to the eucharist and the community (cf. *PO*, 4), the eucharist is the fulfilment of preaching and the source and summit of the church's life (cf. *PO*, 5), while the various works of charity, coordinated by the priest, are the practical actuation of preaching and the concrete expression of a deeply rooted eucharistic spirituality (cf. *PO*, 6).[10]

Joseph Ratzinger developed his own theological understanding of the priesthood in the aftermath of the Second Vatican Council, at a time when the very meaning of what it means to be a priest was hotly debated. In line with the council's teaching, he renews the traditional christocentric conception of the priesthood, centred on the celebration of the sacraments, by incorporating what is valid in more recent approaches, particularly the emphasis on preaching God's word and guidance of the community. He does so not by rooting the ministerial priesthood exclusively in Christ's priesthood as described in the Letter to the Hebrews but, more broadly, in the overall mission of Christ, who is simultaneously prophet, priest and king. In his theological and spiritual writings, Ratzinger builds on this fundamental understanding to establish some practical consequences for priestly life. The priest's task is essentially one of acting as a voice for the Word, so that the saving work of Christ may be continued in our time, through the preaching of the Word and the celebration of the sacraments, especially the eucharist. Placing his confidence in Christ, the priest is, despite whatever trials and tribulations may befall him, a man of joy, of that joy which is founded on Christian faith and hope.

10   Cf. Castellucci, *Il ministero sacerdotale*, p. 234.

THE PRIESTHOOD CONTINUES THE MISSION OF CHRIST

The saving mission of Jesus Christ, the divine Son, is the basis for Joseph Ratzinger's theological reflection on the priesthood. Christ's whole being is mission and relationship. Within the Trinity, the Son proceeds from the Father and is co-equal and consubstantial with him. In accordance with the Father's eternal plan, the Son is sent into the world to exercise a ministry of mediation and reconciliation. Assuming human nature, he represents God among men and acts as the definitive mediator, carrying out his mission of reconciling men to God through his preaching, saving deeds and, above all, the paschal mystery of his death and resurrection. Christ's preaching has a 'sacramental' structure, since 'his message carries within it the concrete reality of the incarnation and the theme of the cross and resurrection'.[11] For the church, this structure points forward to the mutual relation of preaching and the eucharist, and to the intimate bond between preaching and witness lived out in suffering.

Although the Letter to the Hebrews speaks of Christ as the supreme high priest, the term 'priest' (Greek: *hiereus*; Latin: *sacerdos*) is not applied to those who exercise various kinds of ministry in the new testament communities. However, we do find a basis for the Christian priesthood in the mission given to the apostles, a mission whose implications for the life of the apostle are so tellingly described by Saint Paul, especially in his two letters to the Corinthians. According to the gospel account, Jesus 'called to him those whom he desired' and 'he appointed twelve to be with him and to be sent out' (Mk 3:13–15). Apostleship is an act of calling, a sharing in the mission of Christ (cf. Mt 10:40; Lk 10:16; Jn 20:21). Those whom Jesus sends as apostles represent what he is himself. To them, Jesus transmits his own power or authority (cf. Mt 10:1; Mk 6:7; Lk 9:1; 10:19) to continue his saving work: 'As the Father has sent me, even so I send you' (Jn 20:21). Theirs is a mission of reconciliation (2 Cor 5:18), involving the forgiveness of sins (Jn 20:23), the celebration of the eucharist (Lk 22:19) and the communication of the Holy Spirit through the imposition of hands (Acts

11   J. Ratzinger, *Pilgrim fellowship of faith*, p. 159.

6:6; 19:6). However, they can do none of this on their own: 'apart from me you can do nothing' (Jn 15:5). Their mission requires them to be in communion at the deepest level of their being with Christ, from whom they receive the necessary power to carry out their tasks. In this, Ratzinger identifies the essential sacramental foundation of the apostleship: 'Sacrament means: I give what I myself cannot give; I do something that is not my work; I am on a mission and have become the bearer of that which another has committed to my charge.'[12] One can only receive what is God's through the sacrament, not by one's own efforts or by delegation from the community.

To emphasise the christological and sacramental nature of the apostolic ministry, Joseph Ratzinger refers to Saint Paul's priestly and liturgical description in Romans 15:15–16.[13] In this text, Paul declares: 'on some points I have written to you very boldly by way of reminder, because of the grace given me by God to be a minister of Christ Jesus to the gentiles in the priestly service of the gospel of God, so that the offering of the gentiles may be acceptable, sanctified by the Holy Spirit.' Paul here describes himself as a *leitourgos* of Christ Jesus, exercising a cultic or priestly service (*hierougounta*) in regard to the gospel. Proclamation of the gospel is not an exercise in religious propaganda, but a priestly, sacrificial action, which brings the old testament sacrificial worship to fulfilment. This cultic event transforms the pagan world, 'in such a way that as renewed humanity the world becomes cosmic liturgy, in which humanity must become adoration of, a reflection of, the glory of God'.[14] While the connection of the apostolic ministry, thus understood, with Christ's paschal mystery and his ongoing eucharistic presence in the church is not explicit, it can scarcely be denied. Like martyrdom, which is understood in liturgical terms as a

---

12   J. Ratzinger, *Called to communion*, p. 115.

13   Cf. J. Ratzinger, 'Eucharist and mission' in *Irish Theological Quarterly* 65 (2000) 245–64, especially pp 261–2. This was originally a paper given at the eucharistic congress of the diocese of Como on 10 September 1997 and presented in slightly revised form on 24 September 1997 at the National Eucharistic Congress held in Bologna. I am grateful to Revd Professor D.V. Twomey SVD for having drawn my attention to this important article.

14   Ibid., pp 261–2.

pouring out of one's life in sacrifice for humanity and thus as a becoming one with Christ's own self-offering (cf. Phil 2:17), and like christian life as a whole, which is intended to be a pleasing self-offering to God embraced in Christ's own offering of himself (cf. Rom 12:1–2), the spiritual foundation of the apostolic ministry must also lie in that 'attachment to the Lord' which unites us with Christ in a bodily-spiritual existence. Paul emphasises that his mission is not a mere community of thinking, willing and doing, i.e., a relationship which is moral and rational in nature, but something more, because it is (as later theology would say) sacramentally based; it is an actual 'becoming one with the sacrificed and – in the resurrection – eternally living body of Jesus Christ.'[15] It is an inclusion within Christ's own paschal self-offering and existence. The unity of the apostolic ministry is clear: missionary activity is not simply situated next to liturgy; rather, 'both constitute a living totality made up of several dimensions'.[16]

Although some features of the apostles' mission, notably those related to the foundation of the church, are unique to it, the new testament clearly teaches that the apostles did transmit the essential core of that mission to their successors. The Acts of the Apostles and the pastoral letters testify to various ministries in the local churches, which gradually evolved into fixed and definite forms. In this regard, Joseph Ratzinger singles out two texts as particularly important. The first is Paul's farewell address to the presbyters or elders of Ephesus (Acts 20:18–35), which contains a comprehensive theology of the presbyterate. The address is basically an outline of the concept of apostolic succession: the bond between apostle and presbyter is shown in the transfer of pastoral authority from one to the other. The office of presbyter is understood as instituted not by Paul but by the Holy Spirit (20:28), and, as such, must be what was later given the technical term 'sacramental'. The presbyters are indeed regarded in a functional sense as overseers, but they are more than that. They are shepherds, situated in the traditional line of sacred ministries formerly exercised among the ancient people of God, Israel, while also connected in the present with Christ, the

15   Ibid., p. 262.
16   Ibid.

Good Shepherd. They continue the apostles' mission to feed the flock and therefore take up the pastoral ministry of Christ himself.[17]

The second text is 1 Peter 5:1–4 which Ratzinger describes as a kind of 'mirror of priests'. In the new testament, this text provides the strongest linking of apostleship and presbyterate. Peter describes himself as a 'fellow elder' (*synpresbyteros*), thus establishing the essential identity of the offices of apostle and presbyter. The theology of apostleship is thus applied to the presbyterate, which creates a properly new testament theology of the priesthood. Furthermore, the idea of shepherd is also applied to the interpretation of the presbyteral ministry. Christ is 'the shepherd and guardian (*episkopos*) of your souls' (1 Pet 2:25). In this way, the term *episkopos* or 'overseer', which is profane in origin, takes on a new theological depth. The bearer of the presbyteral office is linked not only with the apostle via the term *synpresbyteros* but also with Christ, 'the chief shepherd' (1 Pet 5:4), via the term *episkopos*. We may then conclude that by the end of the apostolic era there is a full-blown theology of the priesthood of the new covenant. The episcopal and presbyteral ministries, which continue the mission of the apostles, are ultimately rooted in Christ, the supreme high priest and Good Shepherd.

'IT IS NO LONGER I WHO LIVE, BUT CHRIST WHO LIVES IN ME'

The christological grounding of the priesthood has consequences for the priest's personal spirituality and his manner of carrying out his ministry. Like the apostles, he too must cultivate a deep personal bond with Christ, especially through prayer, study, and imitation of Christ's obedience, humility, truthfulness, generous self-giving and ready availability for the mission to which he is destined. The bond with Christ, which already exists at the deepest level of the priest's being, must be alive in his consciousness and actions. In this way, it gives unity and purpose to his life

17   Cf. J. Ratzinger, *Principles of Catholic theology*, pp 278–9; idem, *Called to communion*, p. 122.

in the midst of the plethora of activities which he is expected to undertake and it confers an inner depth on all that he does.

To avoid the degeneration of priestly life into mere activism, Joseph Ratzinger emphasises the importance of prayer and contemplation which, apart from restoring our joy in the Lord, are the most important of truly pastoral activities.[18] Acceptance of the priestly vocation and maturation in the priesthood require accompanying Jesus into the hills, the place of his prayer: they entail 'becoming free of the trammels of everyday life, silence, recollection, turning to the living God' in order to arrive 'at that openness and those heights where Jesus' voice can be heard'.[19] A fruitful priestly life is possible only if one has learned to hear the voice of Jesus. In his first meeting with the clergy of Rome, Pope Benedict repeated this conviction: 'spending time in God's presence in prayer is a real pastoral priority; it is not an addition to pastoral work: being before the Lord is a pastoral priority and, in the final analysis, the most important'.[20]

The priest is both the Lord's servant and friend; his life is thus determined by a relationship to Christ which exists at the depths of his being and is at the same time profoundly personal. At the ontological level, the priest belongs to Christ by virtue of what later theology called the 'indelible character', which accompanies the sacrament of orders, affects his being at the deepest level and is the presupposition for the valid celebration of the sacraments. The notion of character expresses a fellowship of service and shows, on the one hand, how ultimately it is the Lord himself who is always acting and how, on the other, in the visible church he nonetheless always acts through men. Since it is Christ who acts through the priest in the celebration of the sacraments, the character guarantees the validity of the sacrament even when the servant is unworthy, but it is also a judgment upon that servant and a demand for living out the sacrament.[21]

At the personal level, Joseph Ratzinger stresses the need for the priest to

18   Cf. J. Ratzinger, *Pilgrim fellowship of faith*, pp 168–72.
19   J. Ratzinger, *Ministers of your joy*, p. 83 (slightly modified).
20   Benedict XVI, Address to the Clergy of the Diocese of Rome, *L'Osservatore Romano*, 18 May 2005.
21   Cf. J. Ratzinger, *Pilgrim fellowship of faith*, pp 162–4.

cultivate a relationship of friendship with Christ. This friendship, accompanied by obedience to Christ's will is, in fact, the secret of holiness.[22] In his preaching and ministry, the priest has the task of making himself a voice for the Word. This service entails an intimate and privileged sharing in Christ's mission, which reveals both the greatness and the humbleness of priestly service. The mission is not the priest's but Christ's, yet the priest shares in the joy of this mission as a friend, for Christ has made his servants his friends (cf. Jn 15:15). Friendship involves trust and Christ entrusts himself in a special way to priests, since they are enabled to speak with his 'I', *in persona Christi capitis*. Friendship with Jesus Christ is 'the core of the priesthood'; it calls for a prayerful relationship with Christ and a deep inner communion with him.[23] This friendship, like all true friendships, involves a sharing of thoughts, sentiments, will and actions, and it enables the priest to live, suffer and act with Christ and for him.

The priest's relationship to Christ is, in turn, the basis of his relationship to the church and the community. As servant, he is called to proclaim not himself nor his own opinions but Christ. Words alone do not suffice for this; the very existence of the priest must be dedicated to Christ so that others may come to know the power and the joy of the faith. Communion with Christ leads to a desire to share in his love for all and in his will to save and help them. In loving Christ, the priest discovers how the christian faith alone brings joy and gives meaning to all human realities, and, as a consequence, he desires ardently to share this treasure with others. Priesthood is thus not a private affair but exists in and for the church to continue the mission of the Good Shepherd. Love of the church goes hand in hand with love for Christ, since only in the real communion of the church do we encounter the real Christ.[24]

Rather than teaching a private philosophy of life, the priest is

---

22   Cf. Benedict XVI, Homily at the Vespers with Seminarians, Cologne, *L'Osservatore Romano*, 24 Aug. 2005. P. Raguis OCD has identified friendship with Christ as the core of Pope Benedict's spirituality; see his 'Une foi profondément enracinée dans le Christ' in *Kephas* 17 (2006) 35–44.

23   Benedict XVI, Homily at the Chrism Mass, *L'Osservatore Romano*, 19 April 2006.

24   Cf. J. Ratzinger, *Called to communion*, pp 128–31.

concerned with making the Word of God known and loved, so as to lead all people to truth and holiness, thereby building up the body of Christ, which is the church. This requires considerable self-denial on his part, measured by the standard laid down by Saint Paul: 'It is no longer I who live, but Christ who lives in me' (Gal 2:20). All of this means losing oneself in Christ, which leads to true self-discovery and fellowship with him. In short, the ministry involves the priest's entire being, beyond any and every function, so that all the priest is and does partakes of the dynamic of 'not me' and yet 'wholly me'.[25]

THE PRIEST, MAN OF TRUTH AND JOY

It is not surprising to find that Joseph Ratzinger, who has dedicated his whole life to the service of the truth, should emphasise love of the truth as an essential element of priestly formation. Being truthful brings risks, as is clear from the opposing examples of Pilate and Saint Thomas More. Because of the dangers involved in living up to truth's demands, it is only too easy to lose courage and succumb to the tyranny of group conformity. The French Catholic novelist Georges Bernanos, an author whom Ratzinger frequently cites, dramatically illustrates this danger in his portrayal of Bishop Espelette, the popular society bishop who knows how to say just what will fit the situation and what would be expected of a man in his position. The bishop, however, has ultimately failed in his vocation, since his willingness to conform to current fashions and ideas is a denial of the eternal character imprinted in him.[26]

As Ratzinger affirms, 'the lack of truth is the major disease of our age';[27] indeed, 'the real problem of mankind is the darkening of truth'.[28] Inability

---

25   Cf. J. Ratzinger, *Pilgrim fellowship of faith*, pp 160–1.
26   J. Ratzinger, *A new song for the Lord*, p. 213; cf. G. Bernanos, *L'Imposture* in *Oeuvres romanesques* (Paris, 1961), pp 387–8.
27   J. Ratzinger, *A new song for the Lord*, p. 213.
28   J. Ratzinger, *Truth and tolerance: Christian belief and world religions* (San Francisco, 2004), p. 66.

to stand up for the truth and face the truth about ourselves hampers
growth in personal maturity and freedom, leaving in its wake a dull sense of
failure. At an interpersonal level, it results in unthinking conformity to
prevailing fashions and ideas, which can quickly turn into a tyranny
opposing the truth. In such a situation, all our days turn grey and joy
cannot thrive. In contrast, by living in accordance with the truth, in fidelity
to God and to his revealed law, man 'comes to experience himself as loved
by God and discovers joy in truth and in righteousness – a joy in God
which becomes his essential happiness'.[29] Only in accepting the sometimes
painful truth about ourselves can we become free from ourselves and for
God. Consequently, truthfulness is the solid rock upon which a mature
and joyful priesthood can be built.

Joy has emerged as one of the major themes of Pope Benedict's homi-
lies and addresses. In his earlier writings, the present Holy Father explains
how joy is to be understood.[30] It is not a superficial sentiment of levity but
arises from the very nature of the gospel itself which, far from being a
burden, is truly glad tidings for humanity. Of course, the gospel can be
unsettling, because it forces us to face the truth about our own sinfulness
and summons us to conversion: 'Truth is not always comfortable for man,
but it is only truth that makes him free and only freedom that brings him
joy.'[31] Joy arises from encounter with the love which can never fail, from
knowing that each and every one of us is willed by God, loved and saved by
him, and intended to share eternal life with him. God so loved us that he
gave his Son to die for us, and so we are loved in truth. The gospel thus
gives life meaning and purpose, confers inner harmony, and enables people
to accept themselves and to live with faith and hope through sometimes
extremely difficult situations.

Given this, it is significant that Joseph Ratzinger's rich and inspiring
collection of writings on priestly spirituality should be entitled *Ministers of
your joy*, an expression derived from 2 Corinthians 1:24. As a minister of

29   Benedict XVI, *Deus caritas est* (2005), no. 9.
30   J. Ratzinger, 'Faith as trust and joy – evangelium' in *Principles of Catholic theology*, pp
     75–84.
31   Ibid., p. 79.

christian joy, the priest must first discover that joy for himself and he can only do so by making the gospel message completely his own in that intimate relationship of friendship with the Lord which should characterise his entire existence. Cheerfulness and a sense of humour are an external manifestation of that interior joy which is a sign of God's grace at work in the soul. The priest's joy, which grows in accordance with the generosity of his gift of self to Christ, arises from his trust in the Lord no matter what trials and tribulations he may have to endure, from his confidence that, despite the paucity of visible results, his work will bear fruit for the growth of God's kingdom, and from his awareness that to be a priest is both the greatest demand and the greatest gift. As a minister of joy, his task is to proclaim the joy of the Gospel to the world through word and sacrament, through the witness of his own life and through generous openness to all that the Lord asks of him.

For his life and ministry to be truly fruitful, the priest must leave all things behind in order to give himself without reserve to the Lord, abide with him and be prepared to accept whatever mission is entrusted to him in Christ's body, the church. This self-giving, in the final analysis, is at the root of the church's law on celibacy. However, the priest's generosity is infinitely surpassed by the Lord's. Referring to Mark 10:28–31, Joseph Ratzinger speaks of the rewards of leaving all to follow Christ: 'God is magnanimous, and if we look honestly at our lives we know that he has in fact responded a hundredfold to every act of giving up.'[32]

The priest comes into daily contact with the source of his joy in the eucharist. In its various dimensions, the eucharist gives rise to joy: joy for the salvation which the Lord has achieved for us in the paschal mystery; joy at the Lord's abiding presence; joy which arises from the intimate union with him which takes place in eucharistic communion and binds us more closely to the life of the Trinity; eucharistic joy which urges us to mission and commitment to bringing the yeast of the gospel into society and the world at large; joy which arises from the Lord's promise of definitive union with him in eternal life and of which the eucharist is a foretaste and pledge.

32   J. Ratzinger, *Ministers of your joy*, p. 126.

At the school of the eucharist, we learn how to live correctly. When celebrating the eucharist, the priest, since he acts *in persona Christi*, is able to speak with the 'I' of Christ. To become a priest and to be a priest means constantly to move towards greater identification with Christ; this is the path to God and others, the path of love.[33] Through the dialogue with Christ which takes place in eucharistic adoration and through the celebration of the eucharistic sacrifice, the priest experiences and learns to imitate the self-giving love which has overcome sin and death, making it possible for man to enter into the joy of eternal life. For this reason, as Pope Benedict exhorted the priests of the diocese of Rome, every priest should be able to say in truth: 'Holy Mass is the absolute centre of my life and of every one of my days.'[34] The eucharist contains in synthetic form the entirety of the priest's mission; since this is so, priests have the great task and responsibility of always living and witnessing 'to the mystery that is placed in their hands for the world's salvation'.[35]

33 Cf. J. Ratzinger, *A new song for the Lord*, pp 225–6.
34 Benedict XVI, Address to the Clergy of the Diocese of Rome, *L'Osservatore Romano*, 18 May 2005.
35 Benedict XVI, Angelus: 18 September 2005, *L'Osservatore Romano*, 21 September 2005.

God and the problem of being

SEAN FERNANDEZ

IN 2004 MONSIGNOR CAFFARA, the archbishop of Bologna, was interviewed by the newspaper, *Corriere della Sera*, on issues and challenges facing the Church. The archbishop's analysis was that the heart of many of the problems which young people today confront is the apprehension of being, for it is this apprehension which sets the spirit of the human person in motion.[1] It was not an unsurprising diagnosis from a philosopher-bishop. One has only to glance briefly at the writings of Cardinal Connell or the various articles written in his honour to realise that a significant *leitmotif* is that of 'being'. Malebranche, Heidegger, Aquinas *inter alios* are made interlocutors in the debate. It was the question of being which lay behind Connell's criticism of Lonergan.[2]

In this article I shall discuss the approach of three contemporary English theologians to the doctrine of God in light of the problem of being. They represent three approaches to the theological task in our milieu. The three theologians are Fr Cornelius Ernst OP, Fr Herbert McCabe OP and Professor Nicholas Lash, late Norris-Hulse Professor at the University of Cambridge. Ernst addresses himself directly to the issue of being by proposing a new metaphysics. McCabe and Lash do not address it in so direct a fashion, but the problem forms the backdrop to their writings.

How would the three theologians frame the 'problem of being'? They believe that we have inherited a *Weltanschauung* which has been 'infected' radically by a certain diremption of body and mind. This diremption they trace to Descartes. This split makes it difficult for us to understand the

---

1   Interview with A. Cazzullo in *Corriere della Sera*, 2 June 2004.
2   D. Connell, 'Father Lonergan and the idea of Being', *Irish Theological Quarterly* 37:2 (1970) 118–30.

language of the scholastics because we interpret them through Cartesian lenses. Our language is compromised. This development has led to the rejection of classical metaphysics. Thus, the language of being and substance is foreign to the modern. 'Being', 'substance', 'form' and 'matter' belong to the language of another distant country.

'Wittgensteinian Thomism' is an appellation coined by Roger Pouivet[3] and which presents us with a useful label with which to apply to Ernst, McCabe and Lash. Whether it is one which applies equally to them all is a question. Perhaps, borrowing from Aquinas, we find the *ratio propria* in Ernst! Why Wittgenstein? Ernst's, McCabe's and Lash's indebtedness to Wittgenstein – the Wittgenstein of the *Philosophische Untersuchungen* – is obvious. They quote him extensively and make use of such concepts as his '*Sprachspiele*' or 'language games.' Lash perceives affinities between Aquinas' 'formal' and 'material', and Wittgenstein's 'empirical' and 'grammatical'.[4] Ernst suggests that there is a certain kinship between the rôle that 'Being' plays in the philosophy of Aquinas and that 'meaning' has in the philosophy of Wittgenstein,[5] which leads him on to say that 'analogy of being' corresponds to '*Sprachspiele*'.[6]

Fergus Kerr has explored the usefulness of Wittgenstein to contemporary theology in his book, *Theology after Wittgenstein*. In this he contends that Wittgenstein's conception of the human soul would be unobjectionable to Aquinas though it might ring strangely in our own post-Cartesian ears.[7] That this evaluation is not peculiar to Kerr may be seen in a later book, *After Aquinas*, in which he discusses certain studies he did under Ernst on the philosophy of Saint Thomas; in the course of these Ernst subjected them to the discipline of Wittgenstein in order to purge them of

---

3 Cf. F. Kerr, *After Aquinas: versions of Thomism* (Malden, MA; Oxford; Melbourne & Berlin, 2002), p. 21. Kerr takes the term from R. Pouivet's *Après Wittgenstein, saint Thomas* (Paris, 1997).

4 N. Lash, *The beginning and end of religion* (Cambridge, New York & Melbourne, 1996), p. 117.

5 *Summa theologiae 1a2ae 106–114 Vol. 30*, p. xx (Ernst, 'Introduction', *Summa theologiae*, vol. 30, p. xx (Blackfriars edition).

6 Ibid., p. xxi.

7 Cf. F. Kerr, *Theology after Wittgenstein* (London, 1986) p. 4.

the infection of Cartesian thought and to help them to appreciate that which Aquinas meant by the soul.[8]

If there are certain congruencies in the theologising of Ernst, McCabe and Lash, there are also significant differences. Ernst believed the a new metaphysics, the metaphysics of meaning, was needed. McCabe was conservative in his approach which consisted of using the tools of Wittgenstein to explicate the metaphysics and theology of Saint Thomas. Lash's approach finds its inspiration in Newman's critique of the narrowing of the language of theology and in Wittgenstein's *Sprachspiele*: truth finds expression primarily in patterns of behaviour and story and secondarily in statements. As Lash expresses it pithily, 'The forms of Christian discourse are set between the poles of metaphor and analogy, of narrative and metaphysics.'[9] The rôle of analogy and metaphysics is to provide a control for and a check on metaphor and narrative. They show the limits of language and prevent our confusing the metaphorical with the analogical. It is in our stories, our many stories, our endless story-telling that what we are, that what is comes to light. In the following sections I shall sketch something of the direction the theology of these three divines takes.

CORNELIUS ERNST

Ernst's *œuvre* is not large. He consciously sought to do theology in a new key. Ernst did not accept Heidegger's criticism of Aquinas and other scholastics for the failing of onto-theology. However, he believed that a metaphysics of being, that is the language of being and substance, etc., was not one to which his contemporaries could relate. Our metaphysics is in some sense chosen for us; we have to look at the language of our time. The dominant language of our milieu is that of 'meaning' and it was Heidegger who has brought about this sea-change. The rôle that 'Being' and

8 Cf. idem, *After Aquinas*, p. 21.

9 N. Lash, 'Ideology, metaphor and analogy' in B. Hebblethwaite & S. Sutherland (eds), *Philosophical frontiers of Christian theology: essays presented to D.M. MacKinnon* (Cambridge, New York & Melbourne, 1982), pp 68–94 at p. 72.

'substance' played in scholastic philosophies is played, for us, by 'Meaning' and the 'genetic moment'. The modern person finds it hard to relate to the God who is the cause of God's own existence and in whom all determination exists simply and would relate more naturally to God who is the 'Meaning of meaning.'

The life, death and resurrection of Jesus is *the* 'genetic moment', which re-shapes, re-news, destroys and re-builds structures of meaning. It continually re-shapes our language and will continue to do so until the end of time. The event is transcendental, not in that it exists in some place above space and time, but in its effect on all language, in all time and space. The genetic moment gives rise to a new language, to new forms of community and life. Following Heidegger, Ernst says that human work is the way in which the human person makes the world a human world – brings it into human projects. Through God's work in the Incarnation, the life and Paschal Mystery and the formation of the Church, human work also becomes part of a larger project – God's project of making the world his own. As Ernst puts it, 'The Gospel in an intelligible (not necessarily *explicitly* intelligible), active presence of eschatological realities in human forms.'[10]

Among its tasks, theology is called to be attentive to the ontological forms the Gospel message has assumed throughout history. This would involve, for example, not only discussing the difference between Aquinas and Scotus on Being, but plumbing the meaning of those differences in their milieu.

What is the place of the Trinity in this theology? Ernst invites us to plumb the meaningfulness of trinitarian revelation throughout history. One begins with the old testament and takes as one's focus the divine name, YHWH. The meaning of God's revelation of his name involves attentiveness to the events and the community to which the revelation gives rise. This tells us what it means to say YHWH is God. This focus shifts to Jesus in the new testament and the Spirit which he sends. It is an invitation to a continual re-reading which does not stop with the new testa-

10   C. Ernst, 'The ontology of the Gospel', *Thomist* 27 (1963) 170–81 at p. 179.

ment, but expands to take in the Christian tradition and the present moment.

Is Ernst ultimately successful in his project? According to Lonergan, the human person is faithful to the dynamic at play in his being perceptive, intelligent, rational and moral when he seeks to know the 'universe of being.'[11] This is in contrast to my world, 'Heidegger's *Welt*' which has me as its centre.[12] The world of Being is thus much larger than my world. Ernst offers a starting point for a dialogue between theology and the broader world. The metaphysics of meaning offers an *entrée* into the world of Being. It is not a resolution of that problem.

HERBERT McCABE

McCabe was an Aristotelian-Thomist. He seems to have set himself the task of explicating Thomas' answers in as clear a manner as possible making use of Wittgenstein's linguistic palate in order to convey the significance of Aquinas' thought. McCabe writes that the missions of the Son and Spirit are the sacrament of the Holy Trinity. They are the life of the Trinity expressed in time. The concept is similar to Rahner's the economic Trinity is the immanent Trinity and vice-versa, but in language which I find richer. McCabe uses the image of a film projected on to a screen. If the film were to be projected on a smooth, white surface, he image would be fairly faithful to that which is imprinted on the negative. However, if the film were to be projected on to a uneven, discoloured surface or on to rubble, the resulting image would be harder to discern. So it is with the Trinity and this disfigured world. As McCabe writes, 'The story of Jesus – which in its full extent is the entire Bible – is the projection of the Trinitarian life of God on the rubbish dump that we have made of the world.'[13] The language of sacrament establishes the nexus between the events of salvation history

---

11   B. Lonergan, *Understanding and being: the Halifax lectures on insight*, ed. E. Morelli & M. Morelli, rev. F. Crowe et al. (Toronto, 1980, 1990), p. 182.

12   B. Lonergan, *Understanding and being*, p. 182.

13   H. McCabe, *God matters*, 48

and the life of the Trinity. Human history, language, community become sacramentalised, capable of expressing the divine life and allowing us to participate through grace in that life. This is not so different from Aquinas' position as expressed by Emery, 'In other words, in the mission, the eternal procession of the divine person is extended to us, in time, by grace.'[14]

One thing that McCabe's theologising does is to place the locus of the Christian experience of the Trinity in the community and flowing from that, the language which is embedded in the life of the community. Language is itself transformed or rather, since it is finite and historical, is in the process of being transformed; it is this transformation, this sacramentalisation of language, to which the seven sacraments of the church bear eloquent testimony. In the sacramental word there is revealed the change brought about in language through the incarnation: its ability to transform situations, reveal truth and the divine. This sacramentalisation of language also makes possible all human discourse about the things of God. Human beings can talk about God, no matter how falteringly, because God has first made language the medium through which she expresses herself.

As McCabe says, 'We learn a language only in so far as we can communicate in a sensuous life.'[15] Christian language, in common with all language, is not the language of disembodied reality. It finds expression and flows from a life in community. It, like all language, is enfleshed in a shared concrete life. The language of Christianity thus finds expression in the church and in the lives of Christians. One important aspect of this common life is that of equality – another *leitmotif* for McCabe.[16]

Herbert McCabe is not a radical theologian. He did not set out to change the theological landscape. He was an Aristotelian-Thomist at heart who was able to communicate Aquinas' insights into the mystery of God with a wonderful clarity. However, his theologising was enriched with Wittgensteinian insights into the nature of language. Among these insights were the embedded nature of language, that is, its connexion to bodiliness and to shared patterns of behaviour.

14   G. Emery, *Trinity in Aquinas*, trans. varr. (Ypsilanti, MI, 2003), p. 161.
15   H. McCabe, *Law, love and language* (London & Sydney, 1968), p. 81.
16   H. McCabe, *God, Christ and us* (London & New York, 2003), pp 83–4.

McCabe's description of the missions of the Son as the sacrament of his being begotten by the Father, and of the mission of the Spirit as the sacrament of his being spirated by the Father and Son, opens up a world of connexions. It finds further expression in his suggestion that the history of salvation just is the life of the Trinity being expressed in our finite and broken world. These images emphasise the closeness between the life *ad intra* of the Trinity and the revelation of that life.

NICHOLAS LASH

Lash has read extremely widely and draws on the thoughts of many other philosophers and theologians. He brings the work together though in a creative synthesis. His works are peopled by authors such as Kasper, Lindbeck, von Hügel, Buber, Rahner, MacKinnon, Newman *inter alios*. His doctoral thesis was on Newman and that influence has perdured. Newman's influence is apparent in Lash's suspicion of what may be called 'Enlightenment influence on things religious'. Newman's defence of the ordinary layperson's faith against criticisms of superstition because such a person could not justify his or her faith, finds its echo in Lash's own insistence that the safeguard of faith is holiness and that faith is not mere notional knowledge, indeed that such knowledge is a small aspect of the rich complex reality of Christian life and faith.

We are a people of language – language is part of our human nature and shapes the way we look at the world, at ourselves. It shapes the stories we tell. For Lash the primary language of Christianity is narrative, and the Christian faith shows its vitality and universality in the myriad of stories to which it gives rise. The fundamental story is, of course, the story of God's revelation of himself in the bible, but this story shapes other narratives and stories. The heart of the story is encounter and here one sees von Hügel's and Buber's influence. There is the ever-present danger of allowing the story, the institution, the dogma to substitute for the encounter which gave them birth and to which they invite the believer to experience for him- or herself.

Lash sees Christianity as an 'educative project ... in which human
beings may learn, however slowly, partially, imperfectly, some freedom
from the destructive bondage which the worship of any creature ...
brings' (*Believing three ways in one God*, 21). The Christian 'educative
project' offers a framework for interpreting the material of one's life; it
offers the means for developing the story of a life, of a community or
society from the Christian perspective. The story it presents allows one to
create one's own story; it provides a grammar or rules for constructing one's
own story. A large part of the new rules it provides involves learning to use
old words in new ways, for example, love, good and forgiveness.[17] The radi-
calness of this new way of using old words and of seeing things differently is
symbolised by the cross.[18] As a project which engages us it is also not something done once and for all. The project is one of life-long learning and
unlearning.[19]

For Lash the doctrine of the Trinity provides us with a grammar for this
project of learning. We can know that we are speaking truly about the God
of Jesus Christ if it is consonant with a trinitarian grammar. We can only
know that we are living the Christian life if it is consonant with the
grammar of the creed. This grammar involves, for us, a tension. It requires
movement, a perichoresis which is a reflection of the perichoresis of the life
of God. Lash himself uses several images in his books to make his trinitarian grammar less abstruse: 'It should be clear that the pattern of a
doctrine of God which thus seeks continually to sustain the dialectic
between pantheism and agnosticism, presence and absence, identity and
difference, affirmation and denial, and which finds the resources for doing
so in continual reappropriation of the gospel narratives, will be trinitarian
in character' (*Easter in the ordinary*, 172). The pattern is far-reaching.
Pantheism and agnosticism are ways of relating to the numinous and for

17   Cf. N. Lash, *Believing three ways in one God: a reading of the Apostles' Creed* (London,
     1992), p. 77; idem, 'Ministry of the word or comedy and philology,' *New Blackfriars* 68
     (1987) 472–483 at p. 477.
18   Cf. idem, *Theology on the way to Emmaus* (London, 1986), p. 176.
19   Idem, *Holiness, speech and silence: reflections on the question of God* (Aldershot &
     Burlington, VT, 2004), p. 5.

Christians there is something about the darkness of God – the silence from which the Word springs – which is not distant from agnosticism. On the other hand, there is the sense of the Spirit who blows through creation and is more intimate to it than it is to itself which has a certain pantheistic feel to it. The Word is the connexion between the two; he is the One who sheds light on the nexus without in any sense explaining it or taking away the tension. Lash sees metaphysical language as providing a certain critical control over the primary language of theology – the language of story. Story, however, is primary. It is through stories that we give expression to the meaning of the world. It is through stories that that which is comes to light.

CONCLUSION

In the writings of Ernst, McCabe and Lash we have theology done in new keys. All three theologians stand on the shoulders of Aquinas. And all three are much influenced by the linguistic philosophy of Wittgestein. McCabe uses Wittgenstein to help us understand Aquinas. Ernst drawing on Wittgenstein and Heidegger proposes a new metaphysics of meaning. One can see the same currents flowing through Ernst's and McCabe's theology in Lash. All three are very much aware of the milieu in which they live and the 'problem of Being'. And the three seek to develop theologies which will speak to their contemporaries – providing ways which will allow being to flower into light.

The contemporary renaissance of Catholic trinitarian theology: an overview

MICHAEL DUIGNAN

O NE OF THE MOST STRIKING features of Catholic theology during the last decades of the twentieth century has been a significant resurgence of interest in the doctrine of the Trinity.[1] After a prolonged period at the margins of mainstream Catholic theology, the doctrine of the Trinity has recently caught the attention of a significant number of theologians from many of the main Christian traditions.[2] Recognising the doctrine's ability to shed light on the specificity of the Christian vision of God, along

1 A cursory glance at theological publications during the 1980s and 1990s reveals without doubt a new wave of interest in the doctrine of the Trinity not only in Catholic theology but also in Protestant and Orthodox theology. On its tenth anniversary in 1977 the Spanish periodical *Estudios trinitarios* 11 (1977) produced an entire volume devoted to a select bibliography of significant works on the Trinity approximately since 1900 (certain articles are confined to the period 1945–1975/7). Without taking into account the works footnoted in its article on the Trinity in Protestant thought, it lists 554 titles. To celebrate its twenty-fifth anniversary in 1991, the same periodical dedicated an entire volume (vol. 25) to a similar survey of published material on the Trinity from 1976 to 1990. Including, this time, contributions from Protestant authors and studies on the Trinity as a philosophical problem, it ran to 4,463 titles. In addition, one might note that while the French periodical *Recherches de science religieuse* published a bulletin on recent publications in trinitarian theology in vol. 52 (1964) 288–93, it did not publish another one until vol. 66 (1978) 417–60. Since then, however, it has published seven such bulletins in the '80s and '90s: 70 (1982) 379–413; 75 (1987) 451–74; 78 (1990) 97–130, 241–68; 82 (1994) 287–309; 85 (1997) 451–94, 601–24; 86 (1998) 143–64; 87 (1999) 585–621.

2 It is important to note that this rebirth in interest in the doctrine of the Trinity is not only confined to the Catholic tradition but is also strongly characterises current Protestant and Orthodox theology as well. This evidences a growing reciprocity between the different traditions at a theological level and the welcome novelty that genuine insights and developments in one Christian tradition now directly influence the others.

with its potential as a model for proper inter-relations at a human, cosmic and even inter-religious level, many contemporary Catholic theologians have embarked on a concerted effort to rehabilitate and reinstate it to its rightful place at the heart of Christian thought and practice.

The impetus for such a development and the framework within which it eventually took place was prepared for in the nineteen-sixties by theological giants such as Hans Urs von Balthasar and Karl Rahner. They summoned Catholic theology to look anew at the doctrine of the Trinity and to recognise the riches that lie therein. However, it was above all in the fertile theological activity created by the Second Vatican Council (1962–5) that the seeds of the current renaissance of trinitarian thought in Catholic circles were nurtured. Seeds, which have only, recently, began to bloom.

Simplifying things somewhat, certain commentators note how in the immediate aftermath of the Second Vatican Council Catholic theology tended to focus, for the most part, on ecclesiological issues in the sixties and christological concerns in the seventies.[3] They highlight how this led Catholic theologians to reconsider the trinitarian dimensions of the church and Christ and eventually, under the influence of a variety of other factors, precipitated a situation where trinitarian theology rather dramatically came centre-stage in the eighties and nineties.

Before examining the various factors that combined to bring about this recent renaissance of interest in the doctrine of the Trinity, it may prove enlightening to glance at the way the topic was dealt with in the period

3   For a similar view of the development of thought on the Trinity in the aftermath of the Second Vatican Council see W. Löser, 'Trinitätstheologie heute. Ansätze und Entwürfe' in W. Breuning (ed.), *Trinitäte. Aktuelle Perspektiven der Theologie* (Freiburg, 1984), pp 19–45; B. Forte, 'Pensare oggi la Trinità. Due recenti opere di teologia trinitaria,' *Asprenas*, 32 (1985) 211; V. Hahn, 'Gültig von Gott reden. Erwägungen anläßlich von W.Kaspers Buch "Der Gott Jesu Christi",' *Theologie der Gegenwart*, 28 (1985) 115; M. Serentha, 'La teologia trinitaria oggi', *La Scuola Cattolica*, 118 (1990) 90–1. G.M. Salvati, 'La dottrina trinitaria nella teologia cattolica postconciliare' in A. Amato (ed.), *Trinità in contesto* (Roma, 1994), p. 13; A. Stagliano, *Il mistero del Dio vivente: per una teologia dell'assoluto trinitario* (Bologna, 1996), p. 18; G. Greshake, *Der dreieine Gott. Eine trinitarische Theologie* (Freiburg, 1997); J. Prades, 'From the economic to the immanent Trinity: remarks on a principle of renewal in trinitarian theology,' *Commmunio*, 27 (2000) 241–2.

prior to the reforms in theology introduced at the Second Vatican Council. In the pre-conciliar period, the main instruments of theological instruction were the so-called 'theological manuals'. Neo-scholastic in nature, these dealt with the various traditional theological topics in a fixed way. As for their treatment of God, they followed the example given by Aquinas in his *Summa theologia*. Thus, they divided the tract into two parts. The first *De Deo uno* focused on the possibility and limits of human reason as it moves by means of analogy from the works of creation to affirm God as one and to discern his main characteristics. The second, *De Deo trino*, examined the biblical revelation of God as Father, Son, and Spirit and endeavoured to prove how this was perfectly compatible with the existence of one divine essence.

Eager to counter the rationalist criticisms of revelation and religion stemming from the Enlightenment, these manuals understandably tended to focus on the reasonableness of faith and revelation. Consequently, they tended to concentrate on reason rather than revelation and to speak in philosophical rather than biblical terms.[4] From our current perspective one can see how this method had certain inherent limitations. As for the doctrine of the Trinity, the Italian theologian Giuseppe Marco Salvati has drawn attention to five of these.[5] Firstly, scant attention was given to revelation, which was pressed into service in order to support already formulated theological thinking rather than being the foundation and norm on which the entire theological edifice was built on. Secondly, the trinitarian dimension tended to be under-emphasised (if not subordinated) with respect to the essential oneness of God. Thirdly, the two tracts on God tended to be but extrinsically related. Fourthly, the practical dimension of trinitarian faith tended to be overlooked with the result that the Trinity appeared as somewhat irrelevant to the everyday life of the believer. Fifthly, the

---

4 See G.M. Salvati, 'La dottrina trinitaria nella teologia cattolica postconciliare', in *Trinità in contesto*, p. 11; F. Schussler-Fiorenza, 'Systematic theology task and methods,' in F. Schussler-Fiorenza & F. Galvin (eds), *Systematic theology: Roman Catholic perspectives* (Dublin, 1992), pp 33–5.

5 See G.M. Salvati, 'La dottrina trinitaria nella teologia cattolica postconciliare,' in *Trinità in contesto*, pp 11–12.

prevalence of a rather deductive and essentialist mentality tended to reduce the Trinity to a *mysterium logicum et ontologicum* or a sort of 'celestial theorem'. Thus, pre-conciliar trinitarian theology tended to leave us with a Trinity rather removed from the other theological tracts and from the mind and heart of the everyday believer. In time, however, the providential combination of a variety of factors was to provide the context out of which a new approach to the Trinity began to take shape.

The German theologian W. Breuning has argued that the first important influences behind the beginning of a renaissance of interest in the Trinity in Catholic theology came not from the traditional approach to the doctrine itself but from developments in other areas of theology.[6] Outlining the most important of these external influences we might note, first of all, how a renewed interest in biblical studies and biblical exegesis brought theology in general and trinitarian theology in particular into contact once again with the inspired texts and the trinitarian characteristics of the God revealed therein. Secondly, a resurgence of interest in patristic theology evidenced how the early church approached the triune mystery of God from the history of salvation and thus emphasised the intrinsic relationship between christology and trinitarian theology. Thirdly, the liturgical movement drew attention to the church's liturgical life and the trinitarian dynamic of the liturgy. Fourthly, a new ecumenical openness led Catholic theology to be challenged by and welcome genuine insights coming from both Protestant and Orthodox trinitarian theology. Fifthly, in the field of ecclesiology, the Council's insistence on the link between the church and the Trinity, its renewed appreciation for the role of the Spirit in the life of the church and its efforts to move beyond a mere hierarchical and institutional vision of church towards an ecclesiology of communion led theologians once more to the doctrine of the Trinity. Sixthly, in christology, the relationship between Jesus and God came centre stage.[7] As in the new testament and the first centuries of Christianity, theologians began to

---

6   W. Breuning, 'Trinitätslehre', in E. Vander Gucht & H. Vorgrimler (eds), *Bilanz der Theologie im 20. Jahrhundert*, III (Frieburg, 1970), pp 21–36.

7   This can be seen in the work of theologians such as H.U. von Balthasar and W. Pannenberg.

recognise that Jesus' identity and mission can be understood only in light of God and that the Christian God can be fully understood only in the light of Jesus. The Christ-event came to be emphasised as the access-point to God and held up as the key to interpreting the Trinitarian mystery, while the mystery of the Trinity was viewed as the backdrop against which a more rounded understanding of the mystery of Christ was to be developed. In the process both christology and trinitarian theology were greatly enriched.

In addition to these external factors, one might note certain stimuli towards renewal arising from within the discipline of trinitarian theology itself. Two theological giants tower above all other in this area: Karl Rahner and Hans Urs von Balthasar. Although not an entirely new development in the history of theology, Rahner's formulation of his *Grundaxiom* on the identity and reciprocity between the economic and immanent Trinity was to prove to be by far the most significant of these. It forced theologians to pay greater attention to the soteriological dimension of the doctrine of the Trinity, demanded that trinitarian theology embark on a more attentive listening to the Word of God and led to a greater osmosis between the two tracts *De Deo uno* and *De Deo trino*. Similarly, the monumental work of von Balthasar brought the paschal mystery centre-stage as the locus *par excellence* wherein the immanent Trinity reveals and offers itself in the economy of salvation. In this regard Salvati notes that while Rahner may have proposed the 'theoretical premises of renewal' for Catholic trinitarian theology, von Balthasar put forward a 'concrete model of trinitarian reflection, no longer conducted in the limbo of abstract speculation but rather on the living terrain of salvation history'.[8]

The combination of such factors provided the theological context from which the current renaissance in interest in the doctrine of the Trinity in Catholic circles began in the early eighties. This increase in interest in the Trinity is all the more dramatic when viewed against the backdrop of its prolonged period of banishment to the margins of mainstream Christian theology.

8   See G.M. Salvati, 'La dottrina trinitaria nella teologia cattolica postconciliare,' in *Trinità in contesto*, p. 16.

It may be helpful to glance at some of the emerging characteristics of
this new retrieval and rehabilitation of the doctrine of the Trinity. Although
it may seem superfluous, I would like to note from the beginning a
palpable excitement and enthusiasm among many contemporary Catholic
theologians with regard to the doctrine of the Trinity and the vast possibilities inherent in a renewed trinitarian theology. It is an excitement shared by
many of the authors from the various Christian traditions who have
written on the topic in the last years. This is all the more striking when we
recall that slightly over a century before authors such as Kant and
Schleiermacher argued along the lines that 'the doctrine of the Trinity,
taken literally, has no practical relevance at all, even if we think we understand it; and it is even more clearly irrelevant if we realise that it transcends
all our concepts. Whether we are to worship three or ten persons in the
deity makes no difference.'[9] The second point, I consider worthy of note is
the newfound importance of the idea of experience.

One of the most significant developments in contemporary Christian
theology has been a turn towards experience as a necessary factor in the
exercise of theology.[10] In the process, theologians have endeavoured to
bring about a critical co-relation between human experience and the many
articles and doctrines of Christian faith. In continuity with this wider
development, we see contemporary Catholic theologians emphasise over
and over again the need to re-immerse the rather sterile and dogmatic trinitarian theology in experience in order to achieve a more existentially
engaging exploration of the topic. Within this context the Australian
theologian, A.J. Kelly, for example, rephrases the words of T.S. Eliot to
speak of trinitarian theology as an instance of having had all of the meaning
but missing the experience and those of K. Jung to speak of 're-immersing
the classic trinitarian doctrine of Christian faith in the "warm red blood of

9   I. Kant, *Religion and rational theology* (Cambridge, 1996), p. 264.

10   A vast array of literature is available on this topic for a brief synthesis of current opinion
     see for example: D. Lane, *The experience of God: an invitation to do theology* (Mahwah,
     NJ, 1981); G. O'Collins, *Fundamental theology* (London, 1981); J. Wicks, *Introduction
     to theological method* (Casale Monferrato, 1994).

experience pulsating through it'".[11] This, perhaps, is one of the most notable developments within contemporary trinitarian theology, which for so many years tended to focus more on doctrinal correctness than on the relevance of the doctrine to the life of the believer. The religious experience of Christ himself, that of his first followers, of the early Christian community, of Christians throughout the ages and that of Christians in our own day along with its trinitarian dimensions has received renewed attention. Although still a work in progress, one can sense the promise such an effort has for a more existentially attuned and inspiring presentation of the doctrine as the religious interpretation of such experience.

Related to this development is the renewed attention being given to what one might call the 'sources' of trinitarian data. The so-called 'return to the sources' that is evident in recent theology is mirrored to a greater or lesser extent in contemporary trinitarian discussion. Our four authors testify to this. Far from indulging in abstract speculation detached from its roots in the experience of divine revelation, there is a genuine desire and effort to listen to and build upon the data to be gleaned from the scriptural witness, the great Christian tradition and contemporary expressions of Christian faith. Probing investigation into the scriptures both new and old testaments, an analysis of the Christian tradition (both east and west) along with attention to contemporary liturgical celebration and moral practice of the faith is given ever-greater attention. Such attention tends to be more scientific and holistic than the simple citing of 'proof texts'.

A fourth and related point is the current discussion of the so-called immanent and economic Trinity. The topic itself has been taken up by many in contemporary Catholic theology in order to avoid irrelevant and abstract trinitarian speculation and to keep the doctrine of the Trinity firmly rooted in the economy of salvation. Its aim is to highlight how each and every theology of the Trinity must be measured against the normative experience of the triune God in the economy of salvation. Interest in the topic reveals an effort among theologians to grapple within our contemporary context with the questions that provoked the doctrine of the Trinity in

11   A.J. Kelly, *The Trinity of love: a theology of the Christian God* (Wilmington, 1989), p. 215.

the first place: What does God's revelation in history reveal about his eternal being? What does the threefold character of God experienced *pro nobis* in the bits and pieces of life tell us about the divinity *in se*?

A fifth point of note is how of late theologians have turned in particular to the paschal mystery as the high-point of the economy of revelation for insights into the nature of the triune God.[12] This approach has borne interesting fruit in the highly influential work of von Balthasar and in contemporary trinitarian theology in general. Such an approach holds together well the soteriological and existential relevance of the doctrine of the Trinity and provides us with a fruitful context within which to raise the difficult question of theodicy.

Another topic that comes to the fore is the apophatic dimension of trinitarian thought. Contemporary Catholic trinitarian theology also exhibits a distinct return to the economic or so-called kataphatic elements of our knowledge of the Trinity. Coupled with this is a distinct reverence for the ever-greater mystery of the triune God as God is in Godself and in God's revelation in history. The words of the Fourth Lateran Council (1215) ring out: 'between Creator and creature no similitude can be expressed without implying a greater dissimilitude'.[13] While this does not excuse one from a faith-inspired investigation and rational presentation of the topic, it does act as a bulwark against an overly rationalistic approach to the triune mystery and emphasises the value of the subjective, personal, intuitive, experiential, symbolic and affective dimension of our knowledge of God. A corollary of this is, perhaps, the eagerness of theologians to turn to and include the topic of doxology – or praise and worship within their treatment of the doctrine.

The opening of contemporary theology to the other sciences and a new sensitivity towards the topic of culture is mirrored in its exploration of the doctrine of the Trinity. Trinitarian theology is turning for inspiration to the

12 For an interesting exposition and analysis of this trend in trinitarian theology see A. Hunt, *The Trinity and the paschal mystery: a development in recent catholic theology* (Collegeville, 1997).

13 J. Neuner & J. Dupuis (eds), *The Christian faith in the doctrinal documents of the Catholic church* (New York, 1982), pp 108–9.

contemporary cultural and intellectual matrix and is finding additional significant *stimuli*. It is perhaps most of all evident in an eagerness to be part of the current search for a new coherent and interconnected vision of reality at a cosmic, personal, social, political, economic and religious level. Many insist that here above all else the specifically Christian vision of God as triune has something significant to offer humanity – not only as a key to interpreting the divine but also as key to the true meaning of reality in its entirety.

The history of the doctrine of the Trinity cannot be told without attention to the development and redevelopment of the categories of 'person' and 'relation' when it comes to explaining plurality in God. However, in recent years, eminent theologians such as Barth and Rahner have instigated a debate on the contemporary use of such categories. In the process there seems to be emerging, after a period of doubt, a firm belief in the value of such terms. Moreover, it is against the backdrop of such categories that theologians are finding imaginative new ways of dealing with age-old problems such as those of God's relation with the world and the question of whether or not God suffers. This naturally leads on to another significant trend in contemporary theology of the Trinity – a renewed interest in the category of Love.

The category of love not only finds a firm biblical basis as an interpretation of the divine reality in the writings of John but has also been turned to throughout history as theologians have striven to make sense of the reality of the triune God. One might note its ever-increasing role in trinitarian speculation as love and the language of love take centre-stage. There is evidence of a consistent and valuable effort among contemporary trinitarian theologians to re-interpret the metaphysical categories of being and substance from within the concept of love. For the majority this is in no way to deny the importance of a solid metaphysical base. It is rather part and parcel of the search to find a more appropriate metaphysics to serve the uniqueness of the Christian faith. This has many advantages for a theology of the Trinity such as those we have already noted where personalist categories come centre-stage with enlightening results. It can also be seen in contemporary theologians renewed interest in the first and third persons of the Trinity or what we might categorise as a turn to the Father and the Spirit.

While the topic of the first divine person or the Father has always had a prominent place within studies on the Trinity our four authors exemplify how the specific characteristics of the Father have caught the attention of contemporary trinitarian theology with a renewed emphasis. Against the backdrop of a renewed interest in the category of love and personalist and relational categories, the venerable idea of the Father as the ultimate source not only of the divinity *fons divinitatis*, but of everything that is, has come to the fore. In the process, theologians have to struggle, as does Kasper, with the identification of the Father and the old testament concept of God as Yahweh and with explaining how the ultimate source of everything that is also relative within the divine plenitude. Consistent with current developments in this area, theologians return to the original narrative of trinitarian revelation rather than the tomes of philosophy to gain added insights here

The ever elusive third person of the Trinity has caught the interest of contemporary theologians who instead of retreating into the categories of obscurity endeavour to spell out exactly of what the specificity of the Spirit consists. It is important to note how within an ecumenical context the theological problems that have arisen around the *filioque* are being revisited and examined. Not only are theologians endeavouring to spell out of what the Spirit consists at the heart of the Trinity but they are also endeavouring to explain how such an intra-trinitarian situation is mirrored in the work of the Spirit in the economy of salvation. Thereby they endeavour to connect the life of the Trinity with the Christian life lived in the Spirit.

Mirroring a turn in theology in general with regard to the necessary practical import of faith, there is a growing effort among theologians of the Trinity to spell out what the doctrine means in practice. With a similar purpose, though with differing methodologies, contemporary scholars of the Trinity strive to draw out the practical ramifications of the doctrine for Christian identity, thought, theology and every-day life in an effort to facilitate the triune faith having an ever-greater effect on people's lives. Whether they effectively achieve this is another matter. However, we cannot but welcome the growing awareness of this need –which bodes well for a more existentially correct doctrine of the Trinity in the future.

In light of our journey thus far, let us cast an eye towards the future of trinitarian theology. One cannot predict the future of this area of research with absolute certainty. However, our current analysis gives us some indication of the direction in which trinitarian theology is going. The return to the sources and re-immersion of the venerable doctrine within the vital contexts of Christian religious experience both past and present has yet an enormous amount of fruit to bear. In the process, however we must not forget that theology is not just a hermeneutic of the Tradition but also the effort to gain a deeper understanding of the data.

We cannot stop at brute experience alone. It cannot become a smoke-screen to hide our efforts to penetrate the data. Any future student of the Trinity must not shirk from this task in order to glean the meaning of what has been experienced and to express it in a coherent and meaningful way so that it may be affective and effective among contemporaries. Thus a solid metaphysical base must be sought for future speculation in this area. It is perhaps in this context that the categories of love, person and relation will be utilised with enlightening results, with the added bonus of trinitarian theology contributing in a more enlightening way to the never-ending human search for the meaning of being and reality, of human personhood, of salvation and redemption, life and living.

Any future theology of the Trinity will need to pay particular attention to the so-called 'signs of the times'. As with our four companions, far from exhibiting a ghetto mentality, it may find in contemporary cultural, social, economic and scientific discoveries shafts of inspirational light for its own penetration of the trinitarian mystery and may in turn enlighten such contexts with the depths of trinitarian wisdom.

Perhaps one of the greatest seedbeds of possible future development lies within the area of theology itself. This is pointed to in particular by Kelly when he laments the oft 'monodimensional presentation' of the Trinity divorced from other theological topics and calls instead for a renewed focus on the interconnection of the mysteries of the faith.[14]

14   A.J. Kelly, *The Trinity of love*, p. 21.

Within such a context each of theology's particular themes – protology, revelation, christology, pneumatology, soteriology, eschatology, moral theology, spirituality, etc. – would find its focus and hermeneutical key explicitly in the trinitarian mystery of God the Father, Son and Spirit. The end result would be that 'the basic trinitarian symbol of God expands into the whole thematization and praxis of theology'.[15]

In conclusion we might note with hope for the future that the work of recent contemporary theologians in this area will be furthered in a variety of ways so that the distinctive trinitarian *Gestalt* of Christian faith might be evident, made meaningful and have a practical felt import in the everyday Christian life. No more might Rahner be quoted to the effect that 'Despite their orthodox confession of the Trinity, Christians are, in their practical life, almost mere 'monotheists.'[16]

15   Ibid., p. 23.
16   K. Rahner, *The Trinity* (New York, 1997), p. 10.

Index

Compiled by Brad Morrow

166   INDEX

Gallagher, Michael Paul, 9, 10, 61–3
Galot, J., 130n
Gaugin, Paul, 103, 104
Gluckmann, André, 48
Goethe, 30
Gresake, G., 154n
Gunter, Colin, 53

Hagan, John, rector, Irish College, Rome, 16
Hahn, V., 154n
Heaney, Seamus, 24
Heidegger, Martin, 22, 25, 26, 47, 49, 57, 143, 145, 147
Heraclitus, 24n, 35
Hope, C., 117n
Hopkins, Gerard Manley, 33, 34
Hügel, Friedrich von, 149
Hunt, Anne, 53, 160n

Ignatius of Loyola, Saint, 56, 102
Institute of Adult Religious Education, Mount Oliver, Dundalk, 88

John Paul II, 44, 50, 51, 54, 55, 56, 70, 72, 78, 96, 124, 125, 131
Johncox, Louise, 24n
Johnson, Samuel, 43
Joyce, James, 103
Jung, K., 158
Jüngel, Eberhard, 53

Kane, Eileen, 2, 11, 17, 19–20, 118n
Kant, Immanuel, 21, 30, 52, 158
Kasper, Cardinal Walter, 149, 162
Kelly, A.J., 258, 163
Kerr, Fergus, 144
Kubler-Ross, Elisabeth, 90

Lambert, Yves, 49
Lane, D., 258n
Lash, Nicholas, 143, 144, 145, 149–51
Lateran, 4th Council of the, 160
Leahy, Breandán, 11, 45, 17–59, 61
Levada, Cardinal William Joseph, 12, 65, 67–75, 78f

Lindbeck, George, 149
Lonergan, Bernard, 147
Löser, W, 154n
Lubich, Chiara, 53, 58

MacKinnon, D.M., 149
MacNiece, Louis, 22, 24n, 31
Malebranche, 25, 143
Maritain, Jacques, 21, 29
Marmion, St Columba,, 16
Martin, Archbishop Diarmuid, 12, 83–5
McCabe, Herbert, 143, 144, 145, 147–9
McGovern, Thomas, 130n
McGrady, Andrew G., 13, 87–100
McQuaid, Archbishop John Charles, 87
Moltmann, Jürgen, 53
Mooney, Carmel, 118n
Muller, Herbert Joseph, 29
Murphy, Joseph, 13, 127–42

Nagel, Thomas, 40f
National Catechetical Directory for Ireland (forthcoming), 96f, 98
Newman, Cardinal John Henry, 62, 109, 145, 149
Nietzsche, E., 23, 48

O Dalaigh, Gofraidh Fionn, 23n
Ó Murchú, Liam P., 23n
O'Collins, G., 158n
O'Rourke, Fran, 13, 20, 21–37, 39

Pannenberg, W., 156n
Parmenides, 31
Pascal, 32
Paul VI, 54, 77
Periander, 28
Peters, John A., 35n
Pieper, Joseph, 25
Pius IX, 70
Pius XII, 70
Plato, 21, 29, 30, 31, 37
Pontifical College for Migrants, 16
Pontifical Council for the Laity, 16
Pontifical Irish College, Rome, 7, 15f, 19, 77